"*The story of Esperanza is riveting....Within these pages there is no shortage of miracles. It is indeed a prescription for hope.... This book provides further evidence for the truth that powerful and transformational kingdom living is available where faith is sufficient. It was a challenge to both my mindset and my personal practice.*"

–**Dr Richard Swenson**, author of *Margin* and *The Overload Syndrome*

"*Prescription for Hope is an honest and inspiring account of the struggle to provide compassionate health care among the medically underserved and disenfranchised of our inner cities in the name of Jesus Christ. It presents a compelling challenge to Christians to step out in faith to effectively serve those who our society shuns. I strongly recommend it to anyone who is pursuing ministry among the poor, whether or not that involves medical care.*"

–**Dr. Art Jones**, Founder, Lawndale Christian Health Center

"*You have a great story here and it bears repeating on the Hill and elsewhere.*"

–**United States Congressman Joe Pitts**

PRESCRIPTION
for *HOPE*

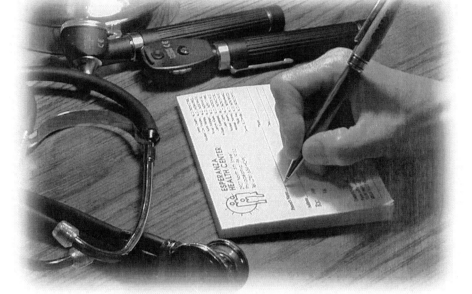

*The Amazing Story
of Esperanza Health Center*

CAROLYN KLAUS, MD

RESTORATION PRESS
Bristol, Indiana

© Carolyn Klaus 2001, 2008, 2010

Printed in the United States of America

ISBN: 978-0-9773643-2-9

Library of Congress Control Number: 2008928649

Table of Contents

Foreword

Iam overwhelmed with writing assignments right now. Nevertheless, the story of Esperanza Health Center is so compelling, and Dr. Carolyn Klaus' involvement such an inspiration to any who know about it, that I felt compelled to give at least a short introduction.

It has been amazing to watch the transformation of many Christians' thinking over the past couple of decades. Whereas once conservative Christians overreacted to the liberal theology that undergirded many who were committed to the social gospel and were suspicious of any attempt to get into social ministries, that has changed. Today, conservative Christians, for the most part, are articulating a holistic gospel that in no way minimizes winning people to Jesus Christ as Savior and Lord, but recognizes that this Savior that they preach has called His people to reach out to those who are poor and oppressed. They are taking scripture seriously and studying it with intensity. They have come to grips with the reality that there are over 2,000 verses in the Bible that call upon the people of God to live out compassion by sacrificially serving the needs of those who, for social and economic reasons, have lost hope.

In recent years, evangelicals have given great attention to one particular verse of scripture. Over and over again, they call attention to what Jesus says in Matthew 25:40. In that verse we read that as we minister to those who are in need, we are reaching out to encounter Jesus. Jesus, the incarnation of the God who created the universe, would overawe us and lay us flat on our faces if He confronted us in all of His magnificence and glory. If Jesus appeared to us in such a fashion, we would be unable to offer Him anything or serve Him in any way. After all, which one of us could look into the face of the King of Glory and say, "There are so many ways I can help you. I know you need me."? Such would be arrogant and foolish beyond anyone's wildest comprehension. Instead, this great Jesus chooses to come to us through those who are in desperate need. He wraps Himself up in those who are poor and oppressed and He says, "Come love me here." He tells us, in Matthew 25:40, that whatever we do to "one of the least of these" we are doing in service for Him.

Over the years, Christians have become cognizant of the need to change the institutions and social structures of America so that they function in just ways that are in accord with the will of God. Today, we know that working for social justice in political and economical spheres is necessary if we are to attack the causes of the hopelessness and despair of the needy people in the world. To this end, many of us, in addition to proclaiming the salvation story of what Christ accomplished through His death and resurrection, are deeply committed to "wrestling with the principalities and powers and the rulers of this age" (Ephesians 6:12). But we also know that Jesus warned us to not be so preoccupied dealing with structural change that we forget that His transformation of society begins from the bottom up. Again and again we must be reminded, as already stated, that He will judge us in terms of what we have done for "one of the least of these." It is so easy for those of us who are social activists to forget that compassionate ministries to individuals are the beginning of transformation on the macro level. Jesus tells us that unless we are faithful in little things (i.e., caring for individuals), we will never be able to handle the big things (i.e., the transformation of social structures). That's a message that can be gleaned from the gospels. While not neglecting the call to address the demonic presence in the "principalities and powers," we must recognize that Jesus really calls for a bottoms-up revolution. The world must be changed by what Tom Sine has called "the Mustard Seed Conspiracy."

A brilliant example of this mustard seed conspiracy can be found in the work of Carolyn Klaus, one of the founders of Esperanza Health Center located in North Philadelphia. This program, which has provided health services to large numbers of individuals from the Latino community in North Philadelphia, has drawn national attention. It became a model for the administration of President George W. Bush as he developed his plans for what has been called the Faith-Based Initiatives. What happened in mustard seed ministries such as Esperanza Health Center inspired the president to make, as a major commitment, his desire to have faith-based programs one of the hallmarks of his administration. While many might point to the failure of the Bush administration to deliver all that was promised when the Faith-Based Initiative was declared as national policy, there can be no question that the President set loose an understanding of how government and faith-based organizations can work together in addressing the most serious problems of the poor, and that future administrations will expand upon that vision and make it an even greater reality. In the midst of all the wonderful things that can be said about Faith-Based Initiatives on the governmental level, it must be remembered that it was in mustard seed programs such as Esperanza Health Center that that vision was born.

As you read this book and learn of the heroic efforts of a committed woman, you will not only see the good that she has done, but more importantly, you will see how Christ has been at work transforming lives. The story that you are about to read is not only a story of how people who desperately needed medical care received it at the hands of this compassionate woman and her associates. It is also the story of how the communication of the Gospel and the power of the Holy Spirit have transformed the lives of so many of those who have entered the doors of Esperanza Health Center looking for healing.

You may already know that the word "esperanza" means "hope." This is a good name for the ministry that was started in part by Carolyn Klaus. The hope that she generated in North Philadelphia is part of a greater message of hope that is breaking loose throughout the world.

I believe that evil has never been stronger or more manifest than it is in the world today, but growing up alongside evil, Jesus tells us through a parable, that His kingdom is also expanding in the world. The destiny of the planet does not lie in the hands of the "evil one," but in the hands of the Lord of history. In the end, He will triumph. As Jesus says in the parable of the wheat and the tares (Matthew 13:24-43), the kingdom of God and the kingdom of evil will grow up together, but in the end His kingdom will endure and the other will be destroyed. This is the great hope for the world, but let us not forget that such social transformation begins in ministries such as that which was brought into being with God's help through Carolyn Klaus and those who worked with her at the Esperanza Health Center.

Tony Campolo, PhD
Professor Emeritus
Eastern University
St. Davids, Pennsylvania

Preface

No one evades the struggle for hope. Sooner or later everyone experiences tragedies beyond repair. Where does a father find hope when police ask him to identify the body of his only child, killed by a drunk driver? Or a violinist who loses her hand in an accident? Or a worker who is fired a month before he was to retire? Or a woman deserted by her lifelong partner?

For a number of years I worked in Latino North Philadelphia. There, as in many American inner cities, hope is in particularly short supply. Many young men must choose between selling drugs and just "hanging out" unemployed—because most of the legal jobs for which they qualify have left the city. Only one in four boys makes it through high school. Some of those who do cannot read. Few expect to get married; three of every four babies are born out of wedlock. Housing is expensive and of poor quality. Most blocks contain abandoned houses. Too many of them have become shooting galleries for drug users. Street violence is routine. Many parents keep their children inside all summer without air conditioning, rather than risk the dangers of bad company or stray bullets outside. Nearly everyone has lost a friend or family member to AIDS. This neighborhood has one of the highest suicide rates in Philadelphia.

If the problem were only "out there," it could be tackled. Generations of enthusiastic helpers, myself included, have sought to change the world, only to discover that the enemy had come "inside the wall." In North Philadelphia I watched leaders' marriages crumble, their health vanish, their good kids go bad. I saw agencies which started well become corrupt. Sometimes the problems seemed to come as attacks from outside; other times people sabotaged their own well-being through character flaws which they seemed unable to change. People who turned to God sometimes experienced a reversal of their circumstances. Sometimes they didn't.

Shortly after this story began, my husband experienced a number of losses which left him profoundly depressed. At the same time our daughter contracted a serious illness. Pray as we might, neither situation changed for many months. A bit later I recognized in myself a workaholism that threatened to destroy my own health and closest relationships. Despite my pleas for divine help and efforts to change, I found myself trapped in my own addiction. Where was God? Why was God not answering our prayers? Strangely, I found hope for my own needs in the process of trying to bring hope to others in North Philadelphia.

Most people in North Philadelphia deal with hopelessness in one of three ways. Some take hope from what may be an excessive belief in human progress. This belief is what attracts many helping professionals to work in the inner city. Unfortunately, when lots of work results in little change, they often get frustrated and burn out.

Others have *no* faith in human progress. Many of these withdraw into their church communities, seeking to protect themselves from the world so that they can "hold out till Jesus comes." This "fortress mentality" has prevented many North Philadelphia churches from impacting their own neighborhoods significantly.

Almost everyone else just escapes—into soap operas, or sex, or drugs, or flashy cars and gold chains, or highly emotional religious experiences with little content. When the escape fails, they live in despair.

My husband and I and a number of friends stumbled onto another approach. Through some serious Bible study it became clear to us that the God of the Bible was concerned about North Philadelphia—and not only about people's *souls* there. Little by little we realized that the Kingdom of God, one of Jesus' favorite topics, referred not only to some future utopia, but also to what this God wanted to do in North Philadelphia now. Believing this, we launched Esperanza Health Center, named after the Spanish word for "*hope*." How it came to be constitutes an epic in itself. Since its opening there in 1989, Esperanza has brought hope to thousands of suffering neighbors through its medical and spiritual care, counseling, social service, and community health education. As its story has spread across the country, it has inspired others wrestling with many different kinds of evil. But hope has also surprised dozens of us who have worked at Esperanza—in ways we had not expected.

Most specifically, my experiences there have given hope to *me* when my personal struggles have seemed overwhelming. Every day at Esperanza I became an eyewitness to God's amazing activity on behalf of people in desperate need. I saw broken lives mended, relationships restored, resources provided out of nothing, supernatural guidance given, locked doors opened, and occasionally, incurables miraculously healed. Gradually it became impossible to believe that the God who was so evident in North Philadelphia was unconcerned about my family's circumstances across town or powerless to change them. God had to be with us, even though He was not doing what we wanted. Eventually we came to understand how God was producing His kingdom in our lives as well.

This is not a comprehensive history of Esperanza Health Center. I tell the story from my own limited perspective. It is the report of how with all my warts, wrinkles, and mixed motives I came to know at Esperanza an amazing God who is completely faithful, infinitely powerful, and altogether good. I pray that through this account others may receive the same kind of hope that I have been given.

Acknowledgements

To thank those who have contributed to the writing of this book is a daunting task.

First, there would have been nothing to write about had not literally hundreds of people from many community groups worked long and hard to give birth to Esperanza Health Center and keep it going. Among these, Living Word Community, a church in central Philadelphia, was central. Its pastoral staff, which at the time included Wendell Sharpe, Ted Lewis, Helen Mesick, Carlos Acosta, and Ron Klaus, by their example led many members of the congregation to make significant sacrifices in order to support the fledgling ministry. Over the years the cumulative sacrifices made by board members, staff, and volunteers of Esperanza Health Center and Summer Medical Institute exceed my capacity to describe adequately.

That their labor had the chance to bear fruit is largely the result of the visionary leadership of the Robert Wood Johnson Foundation, who saw potential in a rather rag-tag group of volunteers and took the risk of providing initial funding to us—even after the particular program through which they funded us had officially closed. To its staff, and in particular, program officer Dr. Terrance Keenan, we are forever indebted.

Several staff members of Esperanza Health Center and the Summer Medical Institute offered particular help during the writing of this book. Dr. Michael Moore shared with me his articles, tapes, and videos on Juan De Jesus. Marialena Gant Zachariah provided me with much of the material used in the chapter on the Summer Medical Institute and corrected my attempts to capture what actually happened. Dr. Ned Rupp gets the credit for some of the street reporting included in that chapter. Scott and Vickylee Moreau, invaluable leaders of the Summer Medical Institute, gave me helpful pointers, useful connections, and strong encouragement as I wrote. Feedback from Dr. Bryan Hollinger was pivotal in convincing me that the project was worthwhile, while Susan Post and Ted Voboril helped push it forward. Special thanks are due the patients who let me interview them and tell their stories here under pseudonyms.

Any literary value in this book must largely be attributed to others. My husband drastically improved every chapter before it left the house. Norm Rohrer gave many useful suggestions. I also am obliged to Joel and Karen Medendorp, who graciously donated countless hours of editing. Later Ruth Ford was professional enough as an editor and enthusiastic enough about the story to fight with me over nearly every chapter. Every fight made me a better writer. I can't thank you enough, Ruth. In addition, Tim and Tari Thiery, Rebecca Musser and Dale Stoll spent long nights proofreading and fine-tuning. Even so, the writing—and any remaining errors—are my own.

Getting a first book published is a long and difficult process. Strong encouragement from Doctors John Perkins, Amy Givler, Art Jones, Judy Shelley, Ron Sider, David Stevens, and Richard Swenson heartened me. Nonetheless, I likely would have given up without the prayer and support of Dale and Gwen Stoll, Harriet Miller, Ray and Barb Miller, Denise Zook, Tim and Tari Thiery, Donna White, David and Kathy Hagen, and Barbara Curlett. I greatly appreciate these traveling companions along life's road. Matt Metz contributed his cover ideas, Jon Morningstar and Lamar Miller their photography talents, and Dale Stoll his know-how in publishing—all precious gifts to me. Words fail me to thank Harriet Miller sufficiently; she poured herself out beyond reason to do the cover and layout within our deadline.

In Chapter 12 I sketch a bit of the impact that Rev. Jim Petty had on my life and on this story. To this day I remain profoundly grateful for the significant movement toward health and wholeness that he helped me make.

To my children, Melody Wilson and David Klaus, belongs my unending gratitude for their patience, long-suffering, and good humor during the years they were growing up when their mom was too busy. That they have each become terrific individuals who have found ways of their own to give to others and who still love me attests to God's grace towards me as much as anything does.

Finally, I cannot overstate my debt to my husband, Ron Klaus, for his contribution to this book, its story, and my life. His digging into the Bible and works of Eldon Ladd and others was what sparked the understanding of the Kingdom of God that gave birth to this effort. He rallied the troops in our congregation to work on the project, and then served those who labored at Esperanza as cheerleader, as board chair, as general contractor. No one will ever know how many of my good administrative decisions at Esperanza came from him. Later he laid down his career to play Mr. Mom at home for many years so that I could give myself to the work at Esperanza without jeopardizing our children. His love beyond measure for me has enabled me to risk, to survive, to succeed, to create, to repent, to grow, to let go, to try again. Esperanza and this book would not exist if it were not for him, and I would be far, far less a person.

However, the real credit for this book must go to Almighty God. This story is His story, begun at His initiative. It has been written with His help and provision every step of the way. May He be honored by the results.

From Darkness to Light

I realized yesterday, with a knot in my stomach, that Juan was leaving us. For days I had haunted the hospital microbiology lab, peering over technicians' shoulders, hunting vainly for an antibiotic which could kill the germs in his bloodstream. Juan had fought hard to live—longer than anyone had dreamed. I knew he was tired. But the nurse's pre-dawn phone call still stung: Juan was dead.

Juan had been more than a patient to me. He was a friend, a valuable co-worker. And he was more—he was now my brother. I sat on the edge of my bed and cried.

For nearly three years I had served as one of Juan's doctors. He had become one of the most powerful examples of transformation I had ever seen. His radiant hope had strengthened me on more than one occasion. Juan had courageously shared his story with other AIDS patients, street people, medical students, suburban church groups, seminary students—anyone who would listen. I remembered it vividly.

♦ ♦ ♦ ♦ ♦ ♦ ♦

Juan DeJesus[1] could not recall a time when his father and uncle were not abusing drugs. Many times he watched as they hit his mother. He never knew what they would do next, and the uncertainty distracted him from schoolwork. Whenever Juan did go to school, he struggled to read and write even his name. Besides, the men in his life had their own idea of education.

"Come on, drink like a man!" they cajoled.

"You're a man! A man has to do what a man has to do!" A real man, they impressed on him, had six or seven children on each corner and a woman on every block.

---

[1] Juan's real name is used here as a tribute to him, and this story is taken from talks he gave publicly. Names of other patients have been changed throughout this book to protect their identity.

Somehow their teaching did not give him much self-confidence. Juan was too shy to talk to anyone.

By the time he was thirteen, he had become tired of standing in the corner at parties. He desperately wanted to be "cool."

One day he discovered that "coolness" cost only a quarter in his Brooklyn neighborhood. A friend bought a two-dollar bag of heroin, and eight young teens got high. In the ensuing weeks, they found that if no heroin was available, they could get almost the same effect from marijuana, cocaine, banana peels, cajona, embalming fluid, glue, or paint fumes. Soon Juan and his friends made sure they got a "hit" before they went to the movies, before they went to school, before they went to a party, and before they talked to girls. Being cool felt great. It never occurred to Juan that he had a habit.

School, he found, was a perfect place to sell drugs. Selling drugs brought easy money and guaranteed excitement. Juan became skilled at his new work. He could tell by taste how good the white powder was: how much sugar and quinine had been added, what kind of sugar it was. He left school still unable to read or write, but on his way to a lucrative career.

◆　◆　◆　◆　◆　◆　◆

Just after his eighteenth birthday, Juan put a needle in his arm for the first time. The high lasted all day and all night. Afterwards, he became frightened and decided to stop using heroin. Within hours he was vomiting uncontrollably, sweating, aching horribly. He had never been so ill. He fought the sickness for a day or so, but soon found himself back at the "cooker."[2] Nothing seemed to matter but getting the precious powder back into his veins. Hopelessly, he realized he was addicted to narcotics. No one he knew had ever broken free from that addiction. He would remain enslaved to drugs for the next twenty-two years.

Now in greater need of a steady income, Juan looked for ways to supplement his drug sales. Gradually he developed a prosperous business as a pimp. He was amazed at how easily he could lure young runaways to work for him. Whenever he wanted to expand his staff, he would hang around

---

[2] A cooker is a flame used to heat a spoon full of water so that narcotic powder can be dissolved in it and made injectable.

New York's 34th Street Port Authority Bus Terminal, watching for a young girl who looked hungry.

"Hey, you want some lunch? How 'bout something to drink?" Gratefully, the girl would talk with him. Over a sandwich, he would gently ask why she had left home. "Didn't your mother let you do what you wanted?" He had a very sympathetic ear. "As long as I'm around, you got no problems." They would walk around the terminal.

"Say, I'd like you to meet a friend of mine." Juan would introduce her to one of his prostitutes, and then walk off a short distance. With a little encouragement, the girl would soon pour out her heart to this new friend. When the prostitute sensed the time was right, she would bring the runaway back to Juan. With her information added to his own keen insights, he would know exactly how to attack the girl's parents. "They sure don't love you!" Or, "Sounds like they didn't give you any freedom!"

If the girl were from a Christian background, Juan saw her as particularly easy prey. Her parents probably had said, "You cannot wear this!" But they likely had not explained why. Juan would take the young teenager to a store. If she wanted a short dress, Juan would buy her two, "real tight," along with lots of make-up. The next stop would be a hairdresser, where the teenager could get her hair done any way she wanted. Soon he would offer her a pill. "Take this. It'll calm your nerves." He would give it to her for a week or two or three, until she had developed a mild drug habit. Meanwhile, perceiving the girl was starved for love, he would croon "I love you," over and over. Soon the girl would be his.

Then Juan would add a condition. "As long as I am around, you are OK. But in order for me to be OK, you need to help me out." By this time, his request would seem reasonable to the young woman. He would put her up in a room and teach her the art of prostitution.

For most of his life, Juan managed a "stable" of at least four or five girls. Through their work, he lived quite comfortably. However, by the mid 1980's, some of his girls and many of his other friends began to die of AIDS.

In 1986, a friend with whom Juan had shared needles got sick. He told Juan, "You'd better get checked, 'cause if you have the virus, there's a new treatment out now that might help you last longer." Juan shrugged it off. "Aaah, I'm all right. My body's strong." Besides, he wasn't gay – he couldn't have HIV. Still unable to read, Juan's only knowledge about AIDS came from his cronies.

To ensure his safety, Juan visited a *"hechicero,"* a Puerto Rican sorcerer. The *hechicero* told him to use some herbs and potions and to cut a finger until it bled. Juan did what he was told, thinking he was safe.

Over the next few years, though, deaths among his girls and bad business deals drained his prosperity. He had despised addicts who stole as a way of life. Now he found himself stealing to support his drug habit. Shopkeepers locked their doors when they saw him. One wintry day he snatched the coats of people attending his mother's church. He even pilfered from his mother, who finally gave up and threw him out of her house.

He had been a flashy dresser; now his reeking clothes went unchanged for weeks. The compulsion for drugs swamped all other desires.

◆ ◆ ◆ ◆ ◆ ◆ ◆

In the spring of 1991, Juan began to feel short of breath, dizzy, and weak. He compensated by using more drugs. Nonetheless, by July he found himself in the hospital, critically ill at only 39 years of age with a mysterious pneumonia. Several days later, his doctor came into his room.

"Juan, I'm sorry to tell you, but you have advanced AIDS. Your immune system is nearly destroyed. You'll be lucky to live six months."

Juan remained very ill despite treatment. Two weeks later he overheard doctors discussing how he might die soon because of fluid in his lungs. That night Juan awoke and began thinking of the God he had dismissed decades before. As a young man he had asked God for help in covering a misdeed. No help had come. He had written God off as a superstition of ignorant people. Now he decided to pray again. "Oh God, if You're there, I'm not asking You to heal me. But please let me know You before I die!" He fell back asleep for the rest of the night.

A couple of days later, his doctor reported, "Looks like the medicine has started to work! You're going to be all right!" Two months later Juan left the hospital.

With Juan's permission, a friend made arrangements to pick him up at noon on the day of his discharge and take him to a rehabilitation program. About 10 a.m. the clerk sent Juan to retrieve his valuables from the hospital safe. Barely able to walk, Juan found himself rushing out to a nearby dealer. By noon he was in the park, stoned again.

As word spread to his family that he had AIDS, Juan learned first-hand the results of misinformation. He first told his mother about his sickness. Tears in her eyes, she reached to hug him, then stopped, paralyzed with fear. He asked if he could stay with her, promising he would not steal. That arrangement did not last long. His mom seemed to believe he was responsible for every itch or sniffle she developed. Juan packed up and moved to the park.

On another occasion he went to a family dinner. Most of his relatives kept their distance, not realizing they were more of a threat to his health than he to theirs. When the meal was announced, Juan looked at his own paper plate and plastic utensils, and at the real china set for everyone else. He sprang from the table and stormed out.

Juan became furious that he had a "gay disease." He had had a variety of sexual experiences, but none of them were homosexual. Memories of his father's voice threatening to kill him should he ever become a homosexual echoed through his mind. He found it hard to look in the mirror. He believed he was cursed. The self-centeredness he knew as an addict now turned to hatred. He hated himself. He hated the people who had given him AIDS. He especially hated people who could run when he couldn't, and people who laughed when he had nothing to laugh about.

Juan decided that if he had to die, he would take as many people with him as he could. During the next couple of months he contaminated hundreds of syringes with his own blood, resealed them in their packages, and sold them for half the usual price to other junkies. He laughed at their desperation. A fellow addict, knowing Juan had AIDS, begged for the needle Juan had just used, then plunged it into his own vein. *Stupid humans,* Juan thought. *Is no price too high for a fix? Is there no other meaning to life?*

◆　◆　◆　◆　◆　◆　◆

One Sunday afternoon in late October, 1991, Juan sat on a park bench, reviewing his options. He needed drugs. His habit now amounted to about $400 per day. He had grown too weak to steal well. He mused, *should I try to get money for one more day's needs, or should I just end it all? It would be fairly easy to hang myself from one of the trees.*

As he was thinking, a sixteen-year-old boy approached. Juan remembered the brass knuckles in his pocket. One blow to the side of the face would put the boy on the ground. Perhaps he would have shoes or a jacket that Juan could grab and sell. Juan prepared to hit the boy. But as he rose to deliver his blow, the boy smiled and said, "Jesus loves you!"

Juan stopped as if he had been slapped. His heart pounded. People had said those words before, and he had laughed them off. For some reason, this time the words arrested him, piercing his soul. He began to sweat. Robbery plans forgotten, he sat down and peered at the youngster. "Oh yeah?"

"Jesus told me to tell you he has a special mission for you." The boy nervously related the simple story of the Gospel. "My father used to be just like you. He had a big drug habit, but look at him now!"

Curious, Juan craned his neck to see the man across the park to whom the boy was pointing.

"Bring him over!" Juan ordered.

In a few minutes the boy's father and cousin were conversing with Juan, sharing how Jesus had enabled them to clean up their lives. "Come on," they pleaded. "We'll get you into a program where you can get straightened out, too!"

"Yeah, I need help, but not right now," Juan protested. "Right now I need a hit." Stuffing their phone numbers into his pocket, Juan strode out of the park.

But Juan could not get the man's words out of his mind: *"You got nothing to lose. 'Cause if you try Jesus and you don't like it, the devil will always take you back."* A couple of weeks later Juan called the man. He would give it a try.

The man took Juan to visit his small Pentecostal church. The church people treated him "like someone special," he later recalled, even though his clothes were filthy and he had not bathed for nearly a month. Juan watched them sing, clap, and jump up and down exuberantly. He reasoned they were high—at least on wine. "Wow," he thought, "they must have something good." He whispered to the man who had brought him, "What they got?"

"They're just worshiping Jesus."

"No. I know they got something, something good. What it is?" As he said this, a woman went forward for prayer. The pastor barely touched her on the forehead when she fell over and began to tremble. "Hey, look," he poked his friend, "give me a little bit of that, but not too much, 'cause I don't know how I'd like it."

"You're going to get more than that!" his friend replied. "Do you want to accept the Lord?"

"Nah, I just want a little bit of *that,* nothing else." Juan had no faith in something he could not explain. But he knew something in this room was real.

Juan's friend turned toward him. "I'm going to pray for you." As he prayed, everyone in the little church joined in heartily.

Afterwards, strangely moved, Juan raised his head. "OK, I'm willing to try it," he stammered. Haltingly, Juan invited Jesus Christ to come into his life. Long afterward, he remembered the cool wave that swept over his entire body. When he had finished praying, he began crying uncontrollably. For the first time in his life, he felt joy.

◆   ◆   ◆   ◆   ◆   ◆   ◆

That night Juan stayed with two new friends. The next day they found him some clean clothes and began looking for a Christian rehabilitation program. In New York, the search proved fruitless. As soon as they described Juan's health condition, each program suddenly ran out of beds. Finally they called Soldiers of the Lord, a small program in inner city Philadelphia, and recounted Juan's needs.

The director asked for Juan to be put on the phone.

"Are you going to give me a hard time?"

Juan promised, "No."

"Are you going to listen to what I tell you?"

"Oh, I don't know," Juan wavered.

"Tell me yes or no!"

"Yes, all right, I'll do it."

"You really want to change? That means, you don't want to use drugs any more?"

"I really want to change. I don't want to do no more drugs."

"OK, you can come, and praise the Lord, we have a bed for you!"

Juan boarded a train for Philadelphia. On the way, he began to scheme. His desire to become drug-free and his understanding of the Gospel were both fairly superficial. He decided to spend a few weeks in Soldiers of the Lord relaxing and getting fat. Then he would shoot back to New York and tell his mother they threw him out.

At Philadelphia's Market Street station, a man with a *Soldiers of the Lord* jacket introduced himself and took Juan to his car. Juan's only "luggage" was a toothbrush given to him that morning. As they approached North Philadelphia, Juan saw drug dealers on the corners. His mouth watered. He thought, *Maybe I don't have to go to New York. I can stay here and get stoned!*

After fifteen minutes, the driver pulled up to the curb. An elevated train roared overhead. Piles of garbage lined the street. Two prostitutes lounged on the sidewalk. A sign on a yellow stucco house welcomed them to "Soldiers of the Lord." It was not quite the vacation paradise he had expected.

That night Juan lay in bed, unable to sleep. About 2 a.m. he began talking to God. "I want to die. I hate the day that I was born. I have never come to nothin' in my life. I have nothin' to live for." He repeated those sentiments, with details, to Whomever might be listening. Around 5 a.m. he began to feel different, cleansed. Again he cried. Again he felt joy.

Nevertheless, life in the rehab program was difficult. Juan had lied all of his life. That habit would not vanish painlessly. Juan had never respected law of any sort. Now he needed to obey even those rules that seemed arbitrary. And it was hard to get along with other residents in the cramped quarters.

Furthermore, he felt he was dying. At 90 pounds, Juan could not climb stairs. Crossing the room took effort. If he got up too quickly, the world tilted. He would go downstairs, hungry for breakfast. He would take a bite, then throw up. When he was able to eat, the sores in his mouth bothered him. He had sores elsewhere that hurt when he used the bathroom. One of his medicines made his face swell up. None of his medicines eliminated his pain. Juan grew distressed. This God that everyone was talking about had not healed him. He thought about leaving. For some reason, he stayed.

◆ ◆ ◆ ◆ ◆ ◆ ◆

In January of 1992, Soldiers of the Lord sent Juan to Esperanza Health Center for a check-up. Juan dreaded the visit. His experience in a New York AIDS clinic had been humiliating. He remembered the thinly veiled contempt on the clerk's face when she saw his Medicaid card and diagnosis. He recalled the superior, distant air of the doctor who handed him pills and walked away.

In the middle of a very busy day at Esperanza, Dr. Michael Moore had only a few minutes to spend with Juan. Dr. Moore realized he had a complicated medical problem, but he also saw Juan's depression. He tended to the immediate need, apologized for the briefness of time, and promised a longer visit the following week. Before Juan left, Dr. Moore handed him a booklet containing scriptures for persons dealing with HIV.

No one had ever treated Juan like this! In other clinics he had felt like a number, a disease. Dr. Moore treated him like a person!

The next week Juan reported that he felt better. The medicines had worked some, but Juan also found encouragement in the words someone read to him from the booklet. Dr. Moore asked if there was anything that particularly struck him. In fact, there was. *"For God so loved the world that he gave his only begotten Son, that whosoever believes in him will not perish but have eternal life."*[3] Juan grabbed that lifeline.

Over the next months Juan and Dr. Moore faced a variety of medical challenges. The kind of immunity affected by AIDS is measured by the number of CD4 white cells in the blood. Normal people have between 500 and 1500 per cubic millimeter. Illnesses known only in AIDS begin to occur when a person's count drops below 200. Under 50, a person is susceptible to nearly every possible infection. Despite the use of all AIDS medicines available at the time, Juan's count stayed under 10 for the rest of his life.

Nonetheless, his physical condition gradually improved. Little by little, he and Dr. Moore developed a complex regime of medicines to control most of his symptoms. They also frequently prayed together that God would be Juan's doctor.

Somewhere along the way, Juan stopped praying to be healed. As he took stock of what he had done to others, he decided he did not deserve to be healed. But he knew that God had a purpose for his life and would preserve him until he had accomplished it.

Exactly that seemed to happen. Month after month, the debilitating complications of AIDS failed to materialize, despite Juan's low CD4 count and the grim prognosis given in New York. Except for a few brief hospitalizations for problems that were easily controlled, he continued to function normally and feel fairly healthy for most of the next three years.

Dr. Moore and Juan confronted non-medical challenges as well. Juan would bring Dr. Moore a letter saying his insurance benefits were being terminated. An outside specialist's receptionist would refuse to give Juan an appointment. The home care service would not provide his required breathing treatment. Sometimes Esperanza's social worker could solve the

---

[3] John 3:16

problem, but often Dr. Moore had to get on the phone as an advocate. Always, they looked to God for His help in breaking the log jams.

Dr. Moore also became an important ally when life in the rehab center was roughest. He appealed to the rehab staff when they did not understand Juan's special needs. He became a sounding board when Juan was frustrated with staff decisions. He gave perspective to help Juan persevere when he was tempted to quit. He encouraged Juan's new dreams of good possibilities for his life.

◆　◆　◆　◆　◆　◆　◆

As the desire for drugs left Juan, an ardent desire to know the Bible replaced it. One of Juan's first answers to prayer came as he was sitting in his room staring at his Bible, wishing he could read. Suddenly the black marks in front of him began to make sense. As he continued to stare, words came into his mind. He began to read – first one sentence, then another, then page after page. He turned to the newspaper lying nearby. It remained gibberish. He told his director about it. "Just keep doing what you're doing!" the director laughed.

Over the next few weeks he applied himself to learning the Bible in English. Within a few months he was reading fluently. Then he began working on the Bible in Spanish. Still unable to read comic books or the newspaper, he enrolled in a concentrated Bible Institute program sponsored by a local Hispanic church. It seemed natural to Juan to read the Bible and pray for two or three hours a day. He now sought the truths of the Bible with the same intensity that he had previously searched for drugs.

One of Juan's favorite verses was Jesus' statement in Luke 5:32: *"I have not come to call the righteous, but sinners to repentance."* Juan had a lot of repenting to do. He worked through a long list of his wrongs—sometimes alone, sometimes with the drug program staff, sometimes with Dr. Moore. As he took personal responsibility, he found God's forgiveness on deeper levels. Though he knew God had forgiven him, he felt remorse for the people he had infected with HIV. He fervently wished he could ask their forgiveness.

Because of the center's location, Juan encountered temptation every day to return to drugs—and the thought always had its allure. Often he would get on his knees behind locked doors, praying for strength to resist temptation. Juan voiced his fear that perhaps, if God healed him, he would "return like a dog to his vomit" to his previous lifestyle. He preferred living with HIV rather than facing this possibility.

◆   ◆   ◆   ◆   ◆   ◆   ◆

After completing his eight months as a student at the rehab program, Juan stayed as a volunteer staff member. Eventually he became assistant director, though without salary except for room and board. Learning to care about people was an entirely new experience. Sometimes it brought tears and pain, but Juan enjoyed counseling and praying with the men who came to him with problems.

He especially liked to encourage men with HIV infection who came into the program. "Hey, if I could find hope; you can, too!" he would affirm. Noting how healthy he looked, some refused to believe that he had AIDS. Others would say, "If I'm going to die anyhow, I might as well get stoned." Once in a while he would find a person willing to work, to study, to change, to grow. "That person will be all right," Juan told himself.

Without other means of transportation, Juan spent a lot of time walking the streets around the drug program. In each street person, he saw himself before he had come to Christ. Daily he sent up heartfelt thanks for the chance he had been given.

Juan's old gift for talking to street people resurfaced, but this time for good purposes. To the sad-looking girls on the corner he would comment, "Ain't it a nice day?" and then, little by little, "What are you doing here? This is a bad block. What's keeping you from going back home?" He could not buy them lunch, since he rarely had more than fifty cents in his pocket. But some did go home. The others, he hoped, at least had something new to think about.

To those using drugs he would talk about AIDS prevention. Juan particularly grieved over the young people who were starting a life of addiction. Over and over he shared his experiences, praying that one here or there would be ready for change. Sometimes he traipsed over to Esperanza to confide his discouragement to Dr. Moore. "They don't want to listen. They don't want to face reality. They think I'm crazy!"

"Yes, but Juan, do you remember how desperate you had to get before you were willing to listen to God? Do you remember how patient God was with you?"

At least once a week Juan visited patients in the hospital. Sometimes he went on his own initiative; sometimes Dr. Moore or I or other doctors from Esperanza asked him to visit other patients with AIDS, with their permission, for a "pep-talk." We found that many who were far less sick than Juan had practically given up on life. He encouraged these people in ways no healthy person could. Eventually the hospital security guards began to recognize Juan and give him free access to the medical floors.

Two days after one such visit, Juan found himself a patient in the same hospital room he had just visited. When he was sick, he sometimes remembered the terror and pain he had seen in the eyes of a dying girlfriend. He would wonder what lay in store for him. As soon as he could push his IV pole, he fought his blues by calling on other patients with AIDS—sometimes feigning ignorance of the hospital's rules forbidding visits to other floors. He looked back on these hospitalizations as "fun."

When he was not working at the hospital or the rehab center, Juan often experienced intense loneliness. On visiting day other residents' wives and girlfriends came to the center. No one ever came for Juan. Knowing he would die soon, he felt it wrong to pursue a relationship with a woman. It was difficult to establish even ordinary friendships. In most churches, once people knew he had AIDS they would shy away and make excuses not to shake his hand. One church, which Juan gratefully joined, was a big exception.

The other exception was Esperanza. Most of the staff greeted Juan by name and often with a hug. Several chatted with him in the hallway when they had a moment. Fred Estrada, Esperanza's executive director at the time, frequently asked Juan about his work. At least one staff member invited him home for a Christmas party. He told medical students, "At Esperanza I'm part of the family."

Juan welcomed the opportunity to speak on an Esperanza public relations video, even though the day of the taping he was in the hospital. Sitting on the edge of his bed in his hospital gown, he declared to the camera, "When I came to Esperanza, I was *dying*. I was dying with AIDS, depressed. Now I'm *living* with AIDS, not dying!"

◆　◆　◆　◆　◆　◆　◆

Juan became increasingly burdened for ex-drug addicts with AIDS in North Philadelphia. Most existing rehab programs were not structured for people with physical limitations. Nursing homes had long waiting lists. AIDS patients who needed help brushing their teeth and feeding themselves often had nowhere to go. *Where*, thought Juan, *was the Church? Why were Christians so ridiculously afraid of serving their brothers and sisters, when the gay community had educated and mobilized itself so well?*

One day, Juan excitedly shared with the Esperanza staff that a woman in the neighborhood had agreed to let him use her house as a rehabilitation center for AIDS patients. How wonderful, that some people could be cared for and encouraged to trust the Lord during the final months of their lives! Immediately he began interviewing potential staff for the new ministry and collecting bed sheets and towels from church people. A little way into the project, however, he discovered that the proposed financial arrangements with the woman would involve some welfare fraud, a very common ingredient in North Philadelphia transactions. Brokenhearted, he cancelled the deal. He would not do God's work in a way that would dishonor God.

Over the last several months of his life Juan became increasingly discouraged over not seeing his home for people with AIDS come to pass. However, during those months Juan continued to grow in his trust in God, refusing to go back to his old way of life, refusing to give up on life itself through a lengthy and complicated hospital course.

Juan had told medical students earlier, "I don't have no religion. I don't believe that I'm Protestant, or Baptist, or none of that. I don't believe in that stuff. I do follow the greatest teacher in the world. That's Jesus, and He's guiding me. Whatever I do, I do in His name. I don't do nothin' without Him, 'cause I tried it on my own for 27 years and it didn't come out good."

"Everyone's going to die; I just got an earlier appointment. Actually, I'm not going to lose nothing; I'm going to gain....I could die, but I'll still be alive. I don't worry about that no more. I feel deep in my heart that I don't belong to this world. I've got something better up in heaven, and it's waiting for me. The only thing I have to do is put more stock into it. I gotta buy more real estate up there. The only way to do that is to try to save people's lives.... I'm not scared of dying now. I'm not saying that I want to die, but I can live with my disease now. I try to help people. At the beginning I wanted to die because I was going to die. But now when I get up and see the sky, I thank God that I have one more day to get someone else into my house.... That's one thing good: it gives you hope, when you don't have no hope."

I was covering for Dr. Moore the night Juan became very sick. We talked about the treatment options—none of them very appealing. "Let's go for it!" he decided, grinning. We prayed together, then embarked on a difficult treatment regime, in which a breathing tube stole his ability to talk. Those words of hope turned out to be his last. On February 4, 1995, the One who had miraculously preserved him for so long took him to where there is no disease.

◆　◆　◆　◆　◆　◆　◆

A few days later, a hush fell over the small sanctuary as Pastor Manuel Rivera rose to the podium. "We are here today to celebrate the life of Juan DeJesus."

He opened the microphone to those who wanted to say something. Many people responded: doctors, a hospital chaplain, ex-drug addicts, a suburban businessman, a medical student, members of Juan's church, Bible Institute friends, and the director of an AIDS ministry. Juan's mother sat on the front row, quiet. She had borne much abuse from Juan over many years. I wondered if she were amazed at the number of people who had been helped, inspired, and profoundly challenged by Juan.

Dr. Moore recalled a time when someone asked Juan what he wanted people to remember about him. Juan answered without hesitation, "There is a true God, and He lives in me."

If that were true for Juan DeJesus, who could be beyond hope?

I sat on the back row giving my own thanks to God for a larger story of which Juan had been just one part....

Beginning 2

Hands wet with dishwater, I reached to answer the phone.

"Hi, Carolyn, this is John Seaman."

"John Seaman! O my goodness!" I exclaimed, setting down the dishrag. John had been a medical student when he attended our church, Philadelphia's Living Word Community, in the 70's. My husband and I had been close to John and his wife, Karen, and were sad to see them move to Buffalo at the end of his pediatric residency. But things hadn't gone as they anticipated. Now, early in January 1982, I heard John saying, "We will move back to Philadelphia if you can find us a group of Christian doctors that I can practice with."

What could be simpler? How wonderful it would be to have John and Karen back in town!

As soon as I finished the dishes, I hunted up the telephone number of the regional director of the Christian Medical and Dental Society, Dr. Lew Bird. I had not attended meetings for years. My life was more focused on being a mommy and a pastor's wife than on being a physician. However, Lew remembered me from the days of my own internal medicine residency, and he promised to send the full mailing list for CMDS members in the Philadelphia area.

When the list arrived, I got out a map and began plotting the locations of Christian doctors. To my surprise, I found *no* group of Christian pediatricians anywhere in the greater Philadelphia area. In fact, I found no medical practice in Philadelphia that was identifiably and overtly Christian. Many Philadelphia hospitals started out Christian, but they had long since drifted from their Christian moorings. A few doctors on the list worked in the city, but they were mostly hidden in large secular institutions. Perhaps John could join one of them?

That wasn't John's and Karen's cup of tea. They remained in Buffalo. Eventually they developed wonderful ministries that served some of Buffalo's neediest people and sponsored medical mission trips all over the world.

A week after John's call I learned that some Philadelphia churches were getting together to study the city's needs and share resources toward meeting those needs. One workshop would focus on medical ministries. Fascinated to think that perhaps other churches had found ways to combine medical and spiritual care, I called to sign up. The cheery voice on the phone told me about talks scheduled on Hospital Christian Fellowship, on Nurses Christian Fellowship, on a broadly ecumenical health center that was just starting, and on opportunities in the public health department. But no *church*, it appeared, had a health ministry. I put down the receiver scratching my head, having heard myself volunteer to make a presentation on the medical needs of Philadelphia. What had possessed me? I had no idea what they were or how churches could get involved.

Over the next couple of weeks, I visited the Philadelphia Health Department and the public library. I learned that Philadelphia had more medical schools than any other city in the U.S. Yet 31% of our city was classified as "medically underserved." This designation came from health statistics, poverty rates, and the number of physicians present. The infant mortality rates in these areas, especially among non-whites, were up to three times higher than the U.S. average. A baby of color in North Philadelphia had no better chance of surviving than babies in some third world countries. Furthermore, hepatitis, tuberculosis, and other infectious diseases were three to five times as common there as in the rest of Philadelphia.

I also discovered that many poor people did not qualify for Medicaid. According to one study, those who did qualify had to overcome many barriers in the health care system to get appropriate care.

Why had I not learned about these things in medical school? I had grown up believing that poor people in our country could always get adequate medical care through hospital clinics or public health centers.

Vaguely uneasy, I got out the map again. It already had revealed that Philadelphia's medical community lacked a Christian witness. Now I began to see that Christian doctors had distributed themselves in the same donut-shaped pattern as secular health care resources: in a ring around the city with a big hole in the middle. Didn't they know about the huge health needs in the inner city? Scripture seemed to indicate that Christ focused most of His energies on poor people. Why did most Christians I know seek to avoid them? Why didn't *I* have any genuine relationships with needy people?

I thought back on the two years I practiced internal medicine while our daughter Melody was little. I had been pleased to land a job with a prestigious and enlightened group of professionals. Ahead of their time, committed to top-of-the-line whole-person care, these doctors hired a social worker and psychiatrist to work part time in our office with patients who had complicated problems. A surprising number of our patients had needed their services.

But I winced as I recalled patients that all we professionals together couldn't help. There was Antonia, whose tension headaches debilitated her. Alone, without relatives or friends in Philadelphia, she didn't need painkillers and Valium so much as she needed a babysitter for her three children under four, so she could get a few hours to herself now and then. And Benjamin, whose high blood pressure was nearly impossible to control. He had been laid off, and despite great effort, he had not been able to find another job. He was frantically worried about providing for his family. And thirteen-year-old Tanya, who came in to request her third abortion. Our social worker had spent a lot of time with her, with not a bit of change in Tanya's behavior. And James, whose severe bronchitis responded so poorly to antibiotics. We treated him for weeks before we learned his furnace was broken and the temperature inside his tiny house was in the forties.

Effective medical care for the poor clearly had to go beyond what we had provided. It would require caring neighbors and friends who were willing to share their time, money, and spiritual strength. Wasn't the Church supposed to do that?

◆　◆　◆　◆　◆　◆　◆

I put away the map. Of all times, why were these questions arising now?

Only recently had I learned to be content as a pastor's wife. I had dreamed since childhood of being a medical missionary somewhere in "darkest Africa." Slowly I had relinquished that dream, as my husband Ron did not share it. I had also given up my medical practice when Melody was two, so I could spend more time with her and support Ron better. Though I loved the mommy role, it did little to flatter my ego. Nor did my role at church, where I didn't even need to do the kind of organizing and counseling that pastors' wives normally do. Several other women were better at that than I was. Except for an occasional night's duty in the emergency room and service to our family, I had no visible role of importance. At first this invisibility had evoked agony in me, showing me how much of my previous church work and medical practice had been prompted by my own need for significance, rather than any desire to please God. However, gradually I had learned to draw contentment from knowing Him and His love for me, rather than from my "great service." And being content, for once, was pleasant.

Now my questions about unmet health needs in Philadelphia gave birth to lively dinner-table conversations. Quickly Ron and I connected them with what for us was a brand new way of looking at the world that we had been discovering at church.

For the past year and a half, our church had been studying the Kingdom of God, the core topic of Jesus' sermons. Jesus' message was succinct: *"The time has come! The kingdom of God is at hand! Repent and believe the good news!"*[4] We looked to the Old Testament to find out how Jesus and His audience understood the phrase *"the kingdom of God."* We discovered that God intended to be the only King His people would ever have.[5] He gave them a marvelous set of laws which, if they had followed them, would have produced a society of peace, justice, and prosperity.[6] All nations would have been drawn to them to learn how to live well,[7] and eventually all nations would have been blessed.[8] Unfortunately, God's people didn't follow these principles even for a generation. Eventually they saw their nation decimated by surrounding tyrants, as God had warned. Nonetheless, prophets from Moses to Malachi predicted that someday God would send Someone to rule in His name, establishing God's reign on earth.[9] In this new kingdom, God's law would be written on people's hearts,[10] oppression would cease, people would eat the fruits of their labor, and lions and lambs would snuggle peacefully.[11] Jesus' announcement, *"The time has come! The kingdom of heaven is at hand!"* brought these prophecies flooding back into the minds of his hearers. No wonder He stirred up so much excitement!

---

[4] Mark 1:15
[5] I Sam. 8:7
[6] Deut. 28:1-13
[7] Deut 4:6-8; Is. 2:2-3
[8] Gen. 12:3
[9] Deut. 18:18; Is 9;2-7; Mal. 3:1-3
[10] Jer. 31:33,34
[11] Is. 65:18-25

Though the evidence did not take exactly the form people expected, Jesus' life did seem to demonstrate that God's reign had begun. Sick people were healed,[12] multitudes were fed,[13] storms were stilled,[14] demons were cast out,[15] and even a few dead people were raised to life.[16] Strangely, He walked away from at least two opportunities to assume political power[17] because He had a prior agenda. God's reign could not come to the world until it came to human hearts that had been radically changed. At unbelievable cost, Jesus did what was necessary to change human nature.[18] But afterwards, His own resurrection convinced those who witnessed it that He had accomplished His goal, that God had indeed entered human history and initiated His kingdom.[19]

Believing this, many people started living very differently. The apostle Peter, who denied his Lord only a few weeks before, began fearlessly proclaiming that Jesus had conquered death. He also began sharing all he had—and performing miracles. God's reign in him was not yet complete, as became clear years later when the apostle Paul had to confront him about his racism.[20] But he, and others like him, became substantially transformed and accomplished amazing things, just as Jesus had promised.[21]

The power of God's kingdom affected social structures as well. The early church dealt with family issues,[22] distribution of wealth,[23] and ethnic conflicts[24] in such a radically new way that newcomers joined daily. The early Christians did not express God's reign perfectly. But the examples of that reign they had already experienced gave them hope that Jesus' other promises would also come true—that he would come back as King of Kings and rule over the whole world. With that hope, often at the price of their lives, they changed the Roman Empire.

---

12 Mark 1:33,34
13 Mark 6:35-44, 8:1-9
14 Mark 4:35-41; 6:47-52
15 Luke 11:14-20
16 Mark 5:35-43; Luke 7:11-15; John 11
17 John 6:14,15; Luke 19:30-34' John 12:12-16
18 Rom. 5:18-19; II Cor. 5:17
19 I Cor. 15:12, 20-28
20 Gal. 2:11-14
21 Acts 3:1-10; 9:32-43
22 Eph. 5:21-6:9
23 Acts 6:1-4; 10; 15:19-21
24 Acts 2:44,45; 4:32-34;

◆   ◆   ◆   ◆   ◆   ◆   ◆

This perspective had disturbing implications for us. If Jesus' kingdom had really begun, and if we claimed to follow Him as our King, we could not write off our discoveries about Philadelphia's inequalities of health care "as none of our business" or "too overwhelming." Since Jesus was involved in health care during his stay on earth; certainly He had opinions on Philadelphia's health care problems in our day. If He were truly our King, how dared we not find out His will for health care in Philly and do it?

For two weeks, Ron and I wrestled with the significance of Jesus' command to "repent and believe the good news" in the context of what I was learning. If He were really King, we needed to repent of our ignorance of the needs of people around us, of our apathy towards the needs we knew about, and of our fears of involvement in a neighborhood which might be dangerous. We needed to repent of our self-centeredness and our reluctance to tackle a project with high demands. On the other hand, we needed to believe God really could and would do something about the situation, if we asked Him. If God were to hear our repentance and choose to change the situation through such unlikely instruments as us, that would be good news indeed.

The first tiny sign that He might do just that came promptly. During those two weeks someone gave me a copy of a workbook published by Granger Westberg in the early 1970's called *"How to Start a Wholistic Health Center."* Mr. Westberg and his followers started a number of clinics, mostly in the Midwest, in which patients' emotional and spiritual needs were systematically addressed along with medical needs. The centers were located in middle-class neighborhoods and did not address issues specific to poverty, but they provided a fascinating model. I highlighted my way through the book, then sent away for everything else Mr. Westberg had published. Soon I compiled a list of thirty-five questions to answer before I would know whether we could attempt such a project.

The second sign followed immediately. One of the half-dozen health professionals in our church heard about an organization called the Christian Community Health Fellowship, a network of Christian health professionals attempting to provide health care to the poor. They had scheduled their first national conference in Washington, D.C. at the end of January. Intrigued, several of us decided to go.

The conference was much more than I expected. We arrived late, just in time to hear Dr. Janelle Goetchus, founder of the Columbia Road Health Services and an extensive ministry to Washington's homeless population. I still wondered if another health project in Philadelphia was really needed. My reservations crumbled as Dr. Goetchus chronicled the shameful lack of health care available to the poor of our nation's capital, and as a young woman accompanying the doctor told her own stories of frustration and neglect.

During their presentation, John Perkins came down the aisle, climbed over five sets of feet, and seated himself next to me. Dr. Perkins, whose model of Christian community development and racial reconciliation had propelled him to international prominence, was scheduled to give a plenary talk later. I had been deeply affected by a couple of his books. When the presentation ended, we chatted briefly, and I decided to attend his workshop on the last day.

En route to the coffee table at the first break, I was intercepted by a young man who introduced himself as Ted Hewson.

"Are you from Philadelphia?" he queried, looking at my name tag.

Yes, I am," I returned. "Why do you ask?"

"Because I am planning to move there this summer." Ted told me he was completing a Master's degree in hospital administration at Cornell, and he already had applied to an administrative residency program at a Philadelphia hospital.

"Actually," he confided, "the real reason I want to come to Philadelphia is that there is a church there I hope to get involved with. It's called the Living Word Community. Have you ever heard of it?"

"Have I ever heard of it? It's the church my husband pastors!" I gasped.

Six years previously I had requested two things of the Lord if He ever wanted me to go back into medicine. First, I wanted to practice in the context of a Christian community. I wanted to partner with a church that could offer the kind of love, encouragement, and practical care that professionals during my previous practice couldn't give. Second, I wanted to work alongside a skilled administrator who could keep my charitable tendencies from sinking the practice financially. I had already begun to sense God fulfilling my first request as our church moved closer to being the kind of serving community I had dreamed of. Could Ted Hewson be God's answer to my other petition?

I introduced Ted to our team, and we fanned out to cover as many workshops as possible. Between sessions we talked intensely with nurses, pharmacists, physicians, and social workers from both urban and rural settings who had passed up opportunities for material reward to serve Christ among the poor. Their frustrations were palpable, but their joy was infectious. They also answered many of my questions.

My last workshop, addressing board development, was led by Dr. Perkins. The participants had a lively interchange. When it was over, he and I chatted for a few minutes in the hallway. After a bit, he pointed his bony finger at me and pronounced, "Carolyn, God is calling you to start a Christian health center in Philadelphia!" A moment later he turned and walked off.

I stood stunned. Could he be right? Was this God's call for me?

Animated discussion filled our car on the way home, but my head was reeling with the weekend's impact. I shuffled through my notes. All thirty-five of my key questions had been answered. And then there was this blunt declaration by John Perkins. Could I go back to "business as usual" after all this?

The next morning, in a little coffee shop near our home, Ron and I thrashed out the implications of the conference. For three hours we discussed the benefits such a project could have for our church. We knew it was time to begin addressing our city's pressing physical needs, as well as its spiritual needs. Though our congregation was multi-racial and contained both rich and poor, it would be good to have more intense contact with a poor community. Having a project outside of ourselves would help us grow together. Additionally, we might learn something about God's power if we tackled something bigger than we could easily handle.

We talked about the implications for me. Our daughter was now eight; it would not hurt her for Mom to have some responsibilities outside our home. For the first time in my life, I could do medicine without needing to do it. My identity now was neither in medicine nor ministry. We both had always felt God had a purpose for my being a doctor. Perhaps the "mission field" of my childhood dreams was only a subway ride away, right here in our own city! By the time we downed the last cup of coffee, we had concluded that John Perkins was right.

Slammed Doors and Detours

The next week I called the friends who had gone to Washington with me to sound them out about the conference. Each of them advocated our doing a health center in Philadelphia. We decided to see how many others might share our vision. We scheduled a meeting in our living room for the first week of March, and began inviting people who might be interested. From the pulpit, Ron mentioned our dream of starting a health center for the poor. I made cookies and shined up our old coffeepot.

Despite heavy rain, thirty-three people found their way into our living room for the meeting. Several nurses came, along with a social worker, a pharmacist, a physical therapist, two medical assistants, a dentist, a dental student, two or three medical students, several nursing students, a couple of housewives, and three or four pastors from area churches. Those of us who had attended the Christian Community Health Fellowship conference shared what we had learned. I presented a few statistics on the health of Philadelphians and the lack of available care for many. Ron concluded with a couple of verses about God's care for the poor and the Church's opportunity to express that care. Animated discussion followed, while the sign-up sheet circulated. By the end of the meeting, we agreed that we formed a critical mass, enough of a team to go ahead. We named our embryonic organization "Koinonia Health Services," after the Greek word for "people working together in fellowship."

Over the next few weeks, the rest of our little church mobilized for a major evangelistic thrust during the coming summer. Forty of our ninety-five adults volunteered to establish an evangelism team, which meant almost everyone else had to cover the responsibilities the volunteers held as Sunday School teachers, worship team members, and small group leaders. Excitement soared as the volunteers formed five teams, each assigned to a different area of the city. I was a little jealous. However, I knew God had given me a different assignment.

◆   ◆   ◆   ◆   ◆   ◆   ◆

I set about to unearth from within the government bureaucracy the most recent listing of Philadelphia's "health manpower shortage areas." Next, I purchased a huge map of Philadelphia, which stretched over much of our kitchen floor, and highlighted those "shortage" areas in yellow.

While I was pursuing this, Jacque Filbey, a nurse who had attended the conference, made appointments for several of us to visit three Christian health centers in the Washington area. Ted, the health administrator we met at the conference, graduated from Cornell just in time to join us.

We left early in the morning, arriving in Washington about ten. Because Dr. Goetchus had made such an impression on me at the conference, our first stop was the Colombia Road Health Center, where she worked. An outgrowth of the Church of the Savior, this handful of committed Christians was having an amazing impact on Washington's poor and immigrant population.

Next, we visited the Community of Hope. A Nazarene church had bought a dilapidated housing project, rehabilitated it, and moved in a number of church families to live among its long-term residents. The church people had quickly encountered their neighbors' overwhelming health needs and had opened a tiny clinic, manned by a nurse practitioner.

Finally, we toured a small health center across town in a church annex. Here, as at the other sites, we were privileged to talk with the clinic administrator. We asked a lot of detailed questions and even obtained recent budgets, financial statements, and fee schedules.

On the way home we marveled at how much God had done through so few. We also talked about each clinic, discussing the aspects we would like to take into our project.

A few days later, I showed Ted my colored map. He suggested we check out a yellow area near Presbyterian Hospital. We knew and liked the reputation of Presbyterian, which was only ten minutes from my house. A quick drive through the neighborhood revealed a decent-looking house for sale only a block from the hospital. Later that week, Ron, Ted, Jacque, a couple of others, and I walked through the house with a real estate agent. Yes, it would need a little rearranging and rehabilitating, but an attractive medical clinic was not hard to visualize there.

The following week Ted and I met with the hospital president. I felt a little nervous walking in to his beautifully furnished office, but he received us graciously. Of course Presbyterian would like to have us in the neighborhood! And yes, he knew the house we were looking at and thought it would be a fine place for us. He offered several names of neighborhood people and agencies we should contact.

Included among those names was a local community development association that had been active for many years. I discovered it even had an officer designated "Health Coordinator." I immediately made an appointment, and we hit it off right away, despite differences in age and race. I was delighted to hear Alfred's[25] dreams for his community; how he hoped to see people empowered to take better care of themselves. I didn't know a lot about empowerment, but it sounded like exactly the kind of thing we wanted to do. Alfred was equally thrilled about my dreams, approving enthusiastically of the house we were hoping to use. We talked during several visits about how we could link efforts to birth a clinic with deep ties to local churches and community groups, where people would receive care for body, soul, and spirit.

Over several weeks the Koinonia team became convinced that the house we were considering was the best location for our health center. Not having the faintest idea where we would get $40,000, we agreed to the asking price, requesting only to be released from the contract if the property could not be re-zoned as a medical office building. Two days later, the real estate agent informed us that our bid had not been accepted. Bewildered, we dropped our contingency escape clause. Again, our bid was rejected, without explanation. We were baffled. Was the real estate agent refusing to sell us the house because it was multiply listed, and she was hoping to gain all of the commission for herself? We knew this was illegal, but we saw no other explanation.

I stormed up to the neighborhood community development association without an appointment. Perhaps Alfred would know what to do. He wasn't in, but the receptionist invited me to wait for him in their tiny waiting room.

About five minutes later, a well-dressed man in his mid-thirties entered and gave the receptionist some work. Then he saw me and paused. "Excuse me, who are you waiting for?"

"I'm waiting for Alfred. I was told he'd be back shortly."

"I'm the president of this organization. What do you want to see him for?"

"He and I have been talking about a new health center we are planning to start in the neighborhood."

---

[25] Not his real name.

At this moment the door opened and Alfred walked in.

"What's this about a new health center here?" The question was posed to Alfred with more intensity than I would have expected.

Alfred began to explain, but his boss interrupted him. "Why haven't you been telling us about this? Don't you know we don't want no new health center coming in here?" They began yelling at each other, nose to nose. I cringed at some of their expletives, hoping they wouldn't start swinging at each other. I pieced together that the City had promised a decade before to build a million-dollar Health Department Clinic in this neighborhood, but had not done so because of budget shortfalls. Alfred's boss believed our arrival would give the City yet another excuse to renege on their promise. He and Alfred apparently had not communicated very well over the past two months.

I slipped out. Ron suggested over dinner that perhaps we should go to our city councilman, who was responsible both for the Presby neighborhood and our own. We met in his office a few days later, across the table from three leaders of the community development association. During the conversation the association president glared at us and quipped, "Rest assured, your health center WILL NOT open here!" The city councilman offered no help.

On the subway ride home, we pondered his words. Was that a veiled threat of vandalism, or at least of political maneuvers to sabotage our marketing efforts? Ron and I looked at each other wide-eyed. What if the real estate agent *had* sold us the house? We would have been stuck with a building that could never be effectively utilized. In His mercy, God had used a real estate agent of apparently questionable ethics to save us from a sure financial and political nightmare!

Twice more that summer we found attractive, possibly affordable sites, located in areas we thought would be good for ministry. In each case, negotiations broke down at the last minute. We were frustrated, but wary about becoming too upset. God had clearly protected us from one debacle; perhaps He was protecting us from others, as well.

◆　◆　◆　◆　◆　◆　◆

The second Saturday night of September while I was ironing, our phone rang. The caller identified himself as a friend of a former co-worker. He owned a small Medicaid clinic in North Philadelphia, one of the city's poorest areas. The previous day his physician had walked out without warning, leaving 6,000 active patients with no one to see them. Did I know anyone who could help?

I didn't know anyone. As for myself, I was clearly too busy starting a Christian health center for the poor. As I hung up, I heard a Voice somewhere inside me: "But I care about all the oppressed. That owner is being oppressed by that doctor! You help him!"

"But God!" I retorted inwardly. "My family would never consent! Besides, who would do the housework?"

Ron, who had been making a sandwich during the phone conversation, broke into my thoughts. "Carolyn, that's a great opportunity! Think of all you'll learn!"

To my shock, even Melody had no problems with my returning to work full-time. We would just have to find someone to take her to her violin lessons and to take care of the house. Cindy Marotta, one of the evangelism team members, immediately offered to work 20 hours a week for us. I found out later she did so specifically as her contribution to the health ministry. We would pay her, but not nearly what she was worth.

Monday morning I called the clinic owner. An hour later I trudged through the tiny building with him, surprised that he had squeezed an x-ray machine and a pharmacy into such a small space. Grudgingly I agreed to work for him for four weeks. That would give him time to find someone else.

The next few days I learned what a Medicaid mill was. At that time Medicaid reimbursed $11.50 per patient visit, regardless of the time spent. It did, however, pay separately for EKGs, breathing tests, x-rays, and medicines. The clinic could make money and still pay me a fairly decent salary if I confined visits to about seven or eight minutes per patient, ordered lots of tests, and wrote lots of prescriptions.

That was not the way I had learned to practice medicine. Seven minutes did not allow enough time to do a history, let alone a physical, on someone with a symptom like "nausea" or "tiredness," of which there seemed to be epidemics. Furthermore, nearly a third of the patients came in every two weeks to refill their "nerve pills." For most of these, I could find no history on the chart substantiating a psychiatric diagnosis. For some, there was no recorded diagnosis at all. I felt I needed at least to find out why these patients were taking these medicines, often in high doses. Before long I was torn up inside by tales of abuse, isolation, grief, and deprivation. In seven minutes I could barely write a refill order, let alone respond appropriately to these needs. And there was no nurse, let alone social worker, to help care for these patients.

I grumbled throughout my subway ride to and from work each day. Why did God let me get stuck working in this pit? Didn't He understand that I wanted to develop a health center that would serve the poor in a Christian way? That I was going to do it *for Him?*

After awhile, I attempted to refer a couple of patients to my friend, Ann Bacon, a professional counselor whom I trusted. She was willing to reduce her rates, but Center City, three and a half miles away, might as well have been another country for my patients. They didn't know how to get there on public transportation, and they weren't at all sure it was safe to go there.

Next, I tried the local mental health center. I wasn't too sure about the quality of counseling dispensed there, but maybe it was better than nothing. Unfortunately, most of my patients couldn't negotiate the required paperwork.

In desperation, I called some friends on the church evangelism team. After a summer's work throughout the city, they had figured out that the poor areas of the city were more open to the Gospel than the more well-to-do areas. (Maybe if we had read the Bible more carefully, we would have figured that out ahead of time.) Now they were concentrating follow-up efforts in North Philadelphia. Would they be willing to visit some of my patients, listen to them, and perhaps pray with them? That would be more than I could do in the office. They were glad to help.

Before long, I was finding two or three patients every week who were pleased to have a layman from a local church visit them in their homes. Soon my patients were pouring their hearts out to my church friends, who were listening, sometimes crying with them, and occasionally offering biblical advice or praying with them. Often they invited my patients to the follow-up Bible study they had started nearby.

By and by I began getting calls from my church friends:

"Carolyn, did you know Sharon's brother-in-law is selling drugs from her front porch?"

"Did you know Carmen's daughter ran away last week and is still missing?"

"Did you know Amanda's husband has been beating her?"

"Did you know George has had no heat in his apartment all fall, and his landlord won't do anything about it?"

"Did you know Sonia's refrigerator is empty and her kids have no shoes?"

Of course I didn't. My patients didn't tell me those things. Together we schemed to connect these patients with resources. My friends began frequenting the welfare office, police station, thrift shops, and other spots where their new acquaintances could get help. They also made sure my patients kept their follow-up medical appointments with me.

Soon these patients were getting well faster than my other patients. That didn't surprise me too much. What surprised us all was the number who began attending the follow-up Bible study. By December, only half the regular attendees were those who had been touched by the concerts, films, dramas, and door-to-door surveys that forty people had worked hard all summer to put on. The other half came from seven-minute visits with a lonely doctor in a less-than-spectacular clinic.

Slowly it dawned on everyone that health care was a better means of evangelism than anything else we had tried. And I realized I was doing Christian health care among the poor; it just was not all taking place inside the clinic! We had stumbled onto a new model for Christian health care: 20% to be done by the health professionals, 80% to be done by the Church. Somehow, that sounded terribly right.

✦   ✦   ✦   ✦   ✦   ✦   ✦

I stumbled onto something else. Just before Christmas I discovered I was pregnant. Ron and I had badly wanted another child, but I had not had a period since Melody was born eight years before. We had spent a lot of money on infertility treatment. I had finally conceived triplet boys, but developed premature labor in my fifth month and lost them all. A second wave of mourning washed over me a few months later when it became clear that my periods were not going to start again. We dared not use drugs again, now that we knew the risk of multiple births with fertility treatments was not just theoretical. At this stage in our lives, that prospect did not seem like one we should deliberately choose. So, I had faced the fact that I would never have another child.

It had taken a long time for me to let the Lord comfort me, but finally, He had. Very thankful for the gift of my beautiful daughter, I had set sail on a new course, determined to do something else with my life. And now I was pregnant! Unbelievable! Thank you, Lord, for the miracle—but why now?

A few weeks later, while we were praying with a few close friends, one gave what he felt was a word from God. "This pregnancy is not going to stop your medical work for Me, though it will change the timing of that work," he said. His words encouraged me a little.

Day by day the winter got colder and I got more tired. The subway trips dragged out. Despite the good things happening with my patients and the evangelism team, I was not happy. Sometimes I complained to God the entire ride. As far as I could see, my boss had not even begun to find someone to replace me. I felt I had to work extra hard to provide even moderately good medical care for my patients. It was not just the lack of skilled help in the clinic. I also had to get on the phone and plead for my patients any time I wanted a test we couldn't provide in the office. The system was certainly not very friendly to people on Medicaid, or worse, without insurance at all.

During one such phone call I found myself arguing with a surgeon who, I felt, had not done a very good evaluation of a patient I had referred to him.

"How do you think you know so much about this?" he gibed.

"I *am* board certified in internal medicine, if you please," I returned.

"You are?" he shot back incredulously. "What the h___ are you doing practicing there?"

So, poor people are not supposed to have access to qualified doctors?

Somehow I made it through those months. I learned the cost of lab tests. I learned about generic drugs. I learned how to plug patients into resources at the hospital. I learned a lot about Medicaid and the administration of a clinic. I learned where I could legitimately cut corners and where I could milk the system a little to keep the clinic alive. With my prescribing practices, it wasn't doing too well. It was, however, paying me a salary, which was going directly into a "health center" fund at the church.

One morning, while watching the last snow melt on the roofs outside my train window, it dawned on me that this was precisely the experience that was going to make our health center possible! Where else would we get money for start-up costs before our first grant came in? We were accumulating invaluable knowledge about health care in a poor community. Our whole church was discovering whole-person evangelism. Sheepishly, I apologized to God for all of my complaining.

♦ ♦ ♦ ♦ ♦ ♦ ♦

In April, I flew to Chicago for the second annual CCHF conference. I took the little brochures we had made about Koinonia Health Services. The pregnancy, now five months along, had finally convinced me that I couldn't be the only doctor in this project. Hopefully I could recruit another one at the conference.

I set up my little table in the display area and waited. Not one doctor even stopped to talk with me. I hardly noticed a third-year medical student, Mike Moore, or his nursing student fiancée, Pam, who signed up for our mailing list.

Disappointed at my recruiting efforts, I still appreciated the talks. This conference focused on community ownership of health projects. Speaker after speaker described how community people often know their needs far better than outsiders do, and they can solve their own problems better than outsiders can, given the resources. Some speakers pointed to Jesus, who let his patients define their own needs. "What do you want me to do for you?"[26] he asked, and even, "Do you want to be healed?"[27] They also showed how He restored their dignity by sharing the credit for healing. "*You* take up your bed and walk!"[28] "*Your* faith has healed you; go in peace!"[29]

This was brand new to me. I had grown up assuming I had what others needed—certainly with respect to the Gospel. Medical school had only exaggerated this illusion. In fact, I didn't really know what *paternalism* meant, any more than a fish would know the meaning of *water*. Suddenly, I realized we had missed something really basic. We needed to find community leaders to form a governing board and tell *us* what they needed in a health center. We needed to be accountable to *them*.

Sunday morning during our ecumenical worship service, there was opportunity for anyone who wanted to share what God had done that weekend. I finally stood up, admitted my previous blindness to most of what had been talked about, and thanked God for this chance to change direction.

---

[26] Luke 18:41
[27] John 5:6
[28] John 5:8
[29] Mark 5:34

Afterwards, while we were checking out, H. Spees, one of the conference speakers, approached me. "Carolyn, do you remember in the prophet Isaiah's life that God gave him a son named Mayer-shalal-hash-baz? That kid had a prophetic name, which meant something for the future of Israel. Well, I think that baby in your tummy is going to be called, 'The-child-who-caused-the-health-center-to-be-done-right!" I grinned back at him.

◆ ◆ ◆ ◆ ◆ ◆ ◆

That night, Ron and I sat up late discussing all that I had learned. When we finally went to bed, I had a hard time sleeping. I kept feeling abdominal cramps. I finally got up, trundled down to the refrigerator, and poured myself four ounces of wine. My obstetrician had said that would help to stop any premature contractions. With that, I was able to sleep.

In the morning, however, I still felt the cramps. I decided to take our car to work, rather than riding the subway. To my surprise, the doctor who was to replace me was at the office, ready for orientation! I quickly showed her around, and then asked her to see my first few patients. I didn't feel great and thought it might be best just to finish some paperwork. By about eleven, I knew I was really having contractions. I told her goodbye and drove straight to the hospital. By God's grace, I had not yet begun to dilate, as I had with the triplets. For the next four or five days, I lived hooked up to monitors and strong intravenous medicine that made my heart pound. How I thanked God that I could afford good medical care! With the medicines my contractions stopped and the baby inside me returned to his or her usual gymnastics. After six days, I was able to go home, but only to complete bed rest and pills every hour and forty-five minutes around the clock.

The first few days at home, I was glad to relax. Then I had Ron set up a typewriter on a table by the bed, so with minimal exertion I could continue the work of Koinonia. However, even that amount of activity brought back the contractions. Frustrated to tears, I griped, "But God, You don't understand! This is Your work I'm trying to do!" The heavens remained silent. I had to stop. Yet over the next three months, I came to understand that God had given me an unusual gift: a chance *really* to rest, complete with meals, housework, and lots of childcare provided by loving friends from our church community. I decided to enjoy it. I slept a lot, read a lot, learned to love the classical music recordings that a neighbor loaned me, and spent some wonderful quiet time with God. Never in my life had I had that kind of leisure. It would be many years before it ever happened again.

On August 15, only nine days before my due date, the contractions began again. This time, we just let them come. That evening after a smooth labor, the doctor handed Ron our completely healthy son, David Paul, all seven pounds and two ounces of him. Our hearts overflowed in gratitude and praise. God had not forgotten any of my prayers!

Unexpected Dynamite

I had forgotten how demanding—and how delightful—a newborn can be. David was a happy baby except when he was hungry, which was most of the time. For the first three months he nursed every hour when he was awake, and he vigorously expressed his displeasure if I could not meet his requirements. But he also gave rapid returns on my investment. He gained a pound a week, somewhat legitimizing his allegations of hunger. He entertained us all with each new skill he gained. By four months, he had discovered how to kiss, in his own sort of way. As he grew, his intense joy over a flower or our kitten or even a dog's bark in the distance reminded me to slow down and savor the gift of life myself. Every day I thanked God that my husband's salary enabled me to stay home with this child. What a fool I had been to choose not to be home when Melody was a baby.

However, there was still work I could do on Koinonia. Thanks to the Chicago conference, I realized our next step would require a lot of listening to people in the community we would serve. And thanks to our experience with the Medicaid mill, we had concluded this community should be the area of North Philadelphia where the evangelism team was working. The clinic's success would require support from that team and from other local churches with which we were developing relationships. The community was certainly needy enough. It had the highest suicide rate of any of Philadelphia's forty-five neighborhoods. It had some of the city's worst health statistics. And according to the *Philadelphia Inquirer,* the lion's share of drug trafficking in all of southeast Pennsylvania occurred in this neighborhood.

David and I began visiting pastors, agency heads, housewives, and anyone in North Philadelphia who would talk to us. While he played with his toys on elegant carpets and cracked linoleums, I got to know the *barrio's*[30] movers and shakers. I also heard many versions of what was wrong with the health care system.

---

[30] *Barrio* is the Spanish word for "neighborhood."

Surprisingly, no one mentioned a lack of doctors. Allegedly, some were practicing without licenses; others were viewed as less than competent. However, the most repeated complaint was that doctors focused so narrowly on patients' symptoms, they often missed the underlying reason for health problems. (With seven minutes per patient, I could understand why.) Furthermore, because they usually worked in isolation, they were ineffective in connecting patients to resources that were available elsewhere.

While making my North Philly rounds, I got to know the staff of another Christian health center starting up across town. These dedicated Christians were committed to providing the kind of whole person care that is essential in a poor community. They helped me fill in a lot of practical details on my "how to proceed" list. I also attended some of their brainstorming sessions and staff meetings over the next year or two.

From this front-row seat, I witnessed a tragedy. In their enthusiasm to recruit a community-based board, the founders of the health center had appointed several people they did not know very well. Though all of their appointees were members of local churches, they varied in the way they defined "Christian." Some carried personal agendas which had little to do with the organization's mission. Others showed little understanding of biblical principles for conflict resolution. I heard tales of gossip, lies, slander, and even conspiracy. At length, torn apart by rivalry and bitterness, the board disintegrated.

For a time, the health center continued to function under private ownership. Unfortunately, the main doctor had his own ideas of how it should operate, and he refused input from anyone. He especially disregarded the views of the support staff, most of whom lived in the community. A few months later, the center closed in financial collapse. I grieved over this avoidable catastrophe, which set back the work of God in that part of the city for years.

After that experience, I resolved that any board or staff members we would recruit would be persons with demonstrated track records as team players, humble enough to receive criticism, proven to handle conflicts uprightly. They also must understand and buy into the vision God had given us. Perhaps we would be slower in assembling our community-based board, but hopefully we would build a board that would last.

◆ ◆ ◆ ◆ ◆ ◆ ◆

Early in 1984 the Christian Community Health Fellowship leaders approached Ron and me about doing a workshop on evangelism and health care at their Third Annual Conference, to be held in April—in Philadelphia! We were flattered, wondering how our seven-month adventure made us experts on this topic. We put together the best workshop we could.

The Saturday of the conference, we dropped off Melody and David at the babysitters' and lugged our workshop materials to our assigned room. Then we settled in the auditorium for the plenary session with Dr. David Hilton. I was completely unprepared for what I was to hear during the next hour.

Dr. Hilton began by recounting his experiences as a missionary surgeon in Nigeria. For ten years he managed a 150-bed hospital, working perhaps eighteen hours a day. He cured many illnesses and saved many lives, only to see the same people returning with the same diseases or injuries. For all of his heroic labor, mortality rates in his district remained about the same. Finally, disillusioned and exhausted, he returned to the States.

Some time later, he returned to Nigeria. This time he gave himself to recruiting, training, and supporting village women as health promoters. He gave them tools to tackle the five most common causes of death in their towns. To elementary school children, they taught songs about the prevention and treatment of diarrhea. The children sang the songs around their houses, teaching their moms the formula for oral rehydration fluid and enabling them to keep their baby brothers and sisters alive when they got diarrhea. The promoters taught moms to mix peanuts with cornmeal for their children, thus ending protein malnutrition. They showed families how to limit mosquitoes by emptying standing water around their homes, and how to purchase chloroquine tablets to protect themselves against malaria. They immunized children against measles, and they taught moms to care for respiratory infections before pneumonia set in. Within a year, death rates from these five conditions plummeted. Yet Dr. Hilton had not treated a single patient.

I squirmed. I realized what he was driving at. Prevention is better than cure. I had heard that a million times. But that was *not* why I went into medicine. I had trained so I could make brilliant diagnoses, prescribe miracle drugs, and rescue people from imminent demise. I didn't want to pass out doltish brochures on nutrition. Community health education was the most boring of my medical school classes. God couldn't be asking me to do *that,* could He? When the presentation ended, I tore to the front and asked Dr. Hilton to join Ron and me for lunch.

We met in the cafeteria after the morning workshops. I peppered Dr. Hilton with questions, all of which he answered convincingly. Inwardly, I was arguing furiously with God. How dared He call me to lay down my goal of dramatically snatching the poor from the jaws of death—for such a mundane task?

By the end of our meal, the fight was over. Tail between my legs, I asked Dr. Hilton how we could learn more about doing community health promotion, and I scratched down his references. As I washed up, I realized the delay caused by David's birth was serving more than one purpose. Again we had seen that we didn't even understand the questions, let alone the answers. Little by little, God was showing us a much bigger picture than we had imagined.

During break that afternoon, Mike Moore reintroduced himself to me. I hardly remembered meeting him at the Chicago conference. Now he was preparing to graduate from medical school, marry the nursing student who had accompanied him there, and move to Philadelphia. He had decided to do his family practice residency in our great city specifically so he could be involved with our health center. God *had* answered my prayers for another doctor—just not on my time frame!

◆ ◆ ◆ ◆ ◆ ◆ ◆

It took me a while to act on what I learned at the conference. I spent the rest of my Koinonia time that year recruiting board members, completing the legal incorporation process, and applying for tax-exempt status.

In the process, I learned that many people could not pronounce "Koinonia." After hearing about the "Coin-in-Ear Health Center" to be started soon, we opted to find another name. A dear friend of mine suggested "*esperanza*," the Spanish word for hope. That seemed to reflect exactly what we hoped to bring to North Philly. Though we continued to use the name Koinonia for a while, we immediately started the paperwork to legalize "Esperanza Health Center, Inc."

During the year, we also hired Bonnie Garcia Camarda, our gifted church administrator, on a part time basis. She helped with administrative details that were getting beyond me. How thankful I was for the Medicaid mill money stashed away in the church's health center fund!

The following spring, David and I finally flew to Evanston, Illinois. While a close friend cared for David during the days, I attended a workshop sponsored by MAP International on community health development. The thirty-five or so attendees included nurses, social workers, educators, a few doctors, and pastors, many from outside the United States. Together, we wrestled with topics ranging from the Bible's wholistic concept of health to the elements of successful development programs and the principles of behavior change.

The week also gave me my first experience with adult participatory education, which proved to be more effective in eliciting behavior change in *me* than I would have imagined.

We discussed in large groups, worked on problems in small groups, listened to expert story tellers, and acted in role plays. We saw demonstrations, watched films, heard case studies, and participated in question and answer sessions. We even sang together. I will never forget the new words we learned to "Old MacDonald Had a Farm:"

> *Diarrhea is no fun, so follow this advice!*
> *Diarrhea is no fun, so follow this advice!*
> *Wash your hands, wash your hands, before eating wash your hands!*
> *Diarrhea is no fun, so follow this advice!*

(Here key shifts half-tone upwards:)

> *Diarrhea is no fun so follow this advice!*
> *Diarrhea is no fun so follow this advice!*
> *Chase those flies! Chase those flies! Cover food and chase those flies!*
> *Diarrhea is no fun so follow this advice!*

(Then comes the grand finale:)

> *But if you should get diarrhea, here is what to do!*
> *But if you should get diarrhea, here is what to do!*
> *A pinch of salt* (demonstrated using the thumb and two fingers),
> *scoop of sugar* (three fingers and thumb held so as to scoop up

about a teaspoon), *added to a glass of water,*
Every time your tummy runs, drink this special drink!

No wonder the kids in Nigeria managed to teach their moms about oral rehydration therapy!

◆　◆　◆　◆　◆　◆　◆

Before the course was half over, I was convinced that community-based health promotion, utilizing these participatory teaching techniques, provided an incredibly powerful tool for improving health—far more powerful, it seemed, than the curative medicine I had been taught.

That raised some heavy questions. Why was I a doctor anyhow? Perhaps I was in the wrong field. Churning inside, I buttonholed a faculty member and a couple of participating doctors during a long afternoon break. I thrashed out my doubts with them. Little by little they helped me glimpse a view of Kingdom health care that was broader even than health education. They also encouraged me to remember that God doesn't make mistakes. It was good that I was learning about community health education and that I had been somewhat humbled in my role as doctor. Nonetheless, God had a place for me as a doctor in His great kingdom. He would still use me to accomplish His purposes if I would continue to trust Him.

For now, thanks to David, full-time doctoring was not an option for me. But I *could* use my credibility as a doctor to raise people's awareness of the importance of health behaviors. Statistics indicated that most Americans die from causes related to lifestyles. Certainly, this should not be true in churches! If Jesus were really reigning in their lives, would people eat until they were obese? How could people sing "All hail King Jesus," and then destroy their usefulness to Him by not bothering to take their high blood pressure medicines? Could God raise Jesus from the dead, and then not be able to help people break free of nicotine and other addictions? Wasn't it God's will that people learn to manage stress in healthy ways? Maybe it was time to start proclaiming this aspect of His Kingdom.

Back home, I did some hard thinking about health education. The people we hoped to serve had a lot of strikes against them. They were poor and poorly educated. Many adults struggled with reading, or even more fundamentally, with English itself. Most existing health education literature would be of no value to them. Frankly, I wasn't even sure they would trust any outside information source. Most people in poor communities got their health information from their mothers and grandmothers, or from a peer group, or perhaps a local spiritualist healer. Professionals were outsiders who wouldn't easily crack the "them versus us" barrier. How could we get appropriate information to the people who need it? Even if we did, would that help them? Knowing that smoking is unhealthy certainly hadn't stopped most smokers I knew. How could we help people actually change their habits?

I remembered my frustration in trying to get patients to change their diets. No matter what I said, most pretty much ate what their families ate. For teens, it would be what their friends ate. To change a person's eating habits, I needed to influence his or her whole social group—something not likely to occur in a doctor's office.

Another barrier to health education had surfaced in my days at the Medicaid mill. Grinding poverty and abuse made some patients feel helpless, even when they were not. Laura, for instance, had been poor and mistreated since childhood. Though she was bright and attractive, she didn't believe she had any control over her future. Faced with a philandering husband who repeatedly gave her gonorrhea, she refused to make choices that, to me, were obvious. Fatalistically, she reduced her expectations to nothing. She didn't need health education; she needed hope that things could change. Only that hope could empower her to make the decisions she needed to make.

And health education among young people would present its own special challenges. My daughter, Melody, had grown up hundreds of miles from her grandparents. She attended a church with few elderly people. To her, cancer and heart disease were not real – they were things you read about. "By the time I have cancer, they will have found a cure," one of her friends had told me. Young people tend to think they are immortal, but somehow this isolation from end-stage illnesses and a buoyant faith in technology had inflated this illusion.

Even for those to whom health issues were very real, healthy behavior would require the ability to defer gratification. A person would have to see past the instant pleasures of rich foods, tobacco, drugs, and promiscuous sex to the future well-being and vitality that self-control would bring. I hoped I was teaching my own kids to do this. But what about Amanda, the girl I had repeatedly treated for sinusitis at the Medicaid mill? She and her mom had been homeless for over a year, and often they did not know where their next meal would come from. And what about Thomas, whose father repeatedly beat him, his brothers, and his mom? Amanda and Thomas might not think they could count on even having a future, so why shouldn't they grab now what satisfaction they could? These kids would need faith in a future before health education would do them any good.

A recent conversation with Melody haunted me.

"Mom, I'm really scared for my friend Aimee[31]," she confided. "Aimee is sleeping around with some older guys."

"In seventh grade?" My eyes widened.

"Well, that's not even the whole problem. She's not using anything to protect herself. She could get AIDS. And she doesn't seem to care. I asked her what she would do if she got pregnant. You know what she said to me? 'Oh, I'd just kill myself. What does it matter?' "

This girl needed more than faith in a future; she needed belief in life itself, belief that she herself had value. Without this, health education would be a waste of time.

Even in the Church, a "spiritualized" lack of self-esteem was devastating people's health. I saw many Christians who seemed to believe that God cared about their spirits, but not their bodies. I knew that idea grew from Plato's teachings, which took root in the early Church as heresy. Nonetheless, I knew a dozen workaholic pastors who were driving themselves to physical breakdowns to "serve God," and they were praised for it. I knew many more whose overhanging bellies and flabby muscles suggested they were setting themselves up for heart attacks.

Clearly, to teach good health practices without dealing with these underlying issues would be a waste of effort. On the other hand, weren't these spiritual issues that the Church should be well equipped to address? Hope and self-esteem were by-products of experiencing God's love. Self-discipline was a fruit of the Spirit. Didn't Jesus' command to love one another include supporting one another through important life-style changes?

◆　◆　◆　◆　◆　◆　◆

I began using David's naptimes to map out a strategy for participatory community health education. Jacque Filbey, Gail Kimbleton, Eileen Giordano,

---

[31] Not her real name.

and Patty Hewson, all nurses on the Koinonia team, came to help. We designed a seminar in which we would teach for about two hours, do screenings for five common health problems, distribute literature, and serve healthy refreshments. We billed it "Health Education for Abundant Living," or "HEAL."

Ron volunteered our church to be the guinea pig. "You know, Carolyn, we can hardly preach to the rest of the city if we are not living in healthy ways ourselves!"

I remembered hearing at the Evanston workshop that getting an authority figure to endorse a teaching is an effective tool for changing behavior. Beaming at his openness, I threw the ball back to him. "That's a great idea, honey! But you know, a lot of people in this church probably view the Koinonia team as 'health nuts.' They'll just blow off the stuff we say. However, if you, their beloved pastor, were to preach on health the Sunday before the seminar, they might pay more attention. By the way, I just happen to have here an outline for a sermon on health, sort of as a starting point for your thinking. Would you like it?"

He laughed so hard he could not talk for a whole minute. "Are you trying to edge me out of my job? That's OK, I think I can come up with a sermon myself!"

Did he ever! He found so much about health in the Bible that, by the time of his sermon, he had made a few behavior changes on his own—fresh evidence that getting people to teach is one of the most fruitful means of helping them learn.

Ron's sermon certainly affected our congregation. Even before the HEAL seminar the following Saturday, several people told us they were changing their health habits.

We determined to get the church to take ownership of this seminar as much as possible. We knew that the more people invested in the process, the more likely they were to change their behaviors.

Cindy Marotta, whose housekeeping services had made it possible for me to work for the Medicaid mill, was also an excellent carpenter. She made a wooden box perfectly designed for exercise testing. Set up one way, it formed a step the right height for men. Set up another way, it just fit women.

We asked one of our church's best cooks to prepare snacks for break time—and then we worked with her to make sure the food was healthy and attractively arranged. People needed to know that healthy eating could be delicious. She needed to know how to teach good eating habits to others. In soliciting specific food contributions from other women, she enlarged the circle of ownership.

Some of the high school kids were live wires. We persuaded five of them to participate in one-minute skits on nutrition. They may have known nothing about nutrition when they started, but they were experts in at least one aspect by seminar day.

The first would come in carrying eggs and bacon and cheese and would boast of his culinary pleasures and immunity to cholesterol problems. After a minute, he would clutch his chest theatrically, and fall down "dead."

A second would pour additional salt on potato chips before popping them in his mouth, bragging how good he felt despite his doctor's warnings about his blood pressure. A few seconds later he would distort his face and pretend the left side of his body was paralyzed. I was pleased at how well, with a little coaching, a high school student could mimic a stroke.

A third, well padded with pillows, would limp in, complaining about the arthritis in her knees. Munching donuts throughout her speech, she would also lament the vision loss that her diabetes was causing. Her doctor had told her that both her arthritis and her diabetes were related to her weight. "But what can I do? Being overweight is caused by my glands, of course (munch, munch)."

A fourth would review the foods that have natural fiber, and dismiss them in distain. He would sit down *very* carefully, however, on a pillow with a hole in it, explaining to us that his hemorrhoids were acting up.

The last participant, slurping Coke and chewing on a Milky Way, would complain of headaches and difficulty concentrating in school, which the nurse said might be due to too much sugar in her diet. "But that's not nearly so bad as my toothache!" she would say, grimacing to show several teeth blackened out by tape. "What, oh what can I do about my toothache?"

We figured the audience, who loved and identified with these kids, would laugh harder, remember more, and stand a better chance of incorporating that information into their lives through these dramas than through anything we could say.

We also found some non-health care personnel who were willing to teach. Aracelis Gomez, a homemaker, prepared a module on smoke detectors and household poison control. Will Doggett, a college student studying physical education, presented a unit on exercise.

By the Saturday of our first seminar, excitement was high. Seventy people filled our church basement, stuffing the bags we provided with literature and their mouths with apple wedges and broccoli dip. I was surprised at all the people who stepped up and down on Cindy's box, panting, to test their cardiovascular fitness. Almost everyone made it to all screening stations and stayed through all sessions. By the end, almost everyone had made some kind of health decision.

◆   ◆   ◆   ◆   ◆   ◆   ◆

The response to our first effort was so encouraging that we began booking seminars elsewhere. Our volunteer team expanded steadily. Over the next nine months, we did six HEAL seminars in English and six in Spanish, most of them in churches. Several factors made the seminars popular.

First, we let each group set its own agenda. A few weeks before the seminar, two or three of us would meet with the pastor and several lay leaders to listen to their perceptions of health needs in their church. Some groups wanted us to cover stress management; others didn't. Some churches wanted to discuss sexuality, while others were horrified at that idea. Interestingly, some secular groups asked us to talk about what the Bible says about health. We found it was important to address the felt needs of each group.

Second, we insisted that a group participate in its own learning. For example, we would not do a seminar unless someone from the group accepted responsibility for follow-up. We trained and supported that person to stay in contact with those who identified health problems at the seminar. We also made sure someone would be responsible to prepare refreshments, and we worked with that person to guarantee they would model healthy eating within the group's cultural context. I learned about *quenepas* and *guayabanas,* Puerto Rican fruits I didn't even know existed. And we recruited members of that group to do the skits.

Third, we did very little lecturing. Besides the skits, we involved seminar participants by asking questions to draw out their own health knowledge. We introduced some small group problem-solving sessions, where each group designed a healthy menu based on a fast-food diet, a Puerto Rican diet, an African-American soul food diet, or traditional American diet. The groups presented their findings and learned from each other. We also featured testimonials from individuals who had successfully worked through specific health problems.

At the end of each seminar, we asked participants to list three health behaviors they wanted to change. Depending on the group norms, we asked them to share what they had decided to change with their small group or with one other person. Telling someone they would see again made them feel more accountable and increased the likelihood that they would really change. Then, if it was appropriate, we asked them to pray for each other, getting God involved in their contract.

Finally, we asked participants to sign up for the type of follow-up they wanted: perhaps an overeater's group, an exercise group, or a class on parenting techniques. We then worked with the follow-up coordinator to develop those resources within the group.

When we were able to do all of this, the power for behavior change amazed us. For instance, the seminar deeply impacted the Spanish congregation affiliated with our church. Pastor Carlos Acosta began a weight-lifting group in his basement. Several people started their own version of Weight-Watchers. I saw others jogging together as I drove through their neighborhood. People brought fruit, rather than cakes and pies, to our church potlucks. Bonnie told me, chuckling, how the person who brought donuts to the Saturday morning teacher's meeting was gently but firmly corrected. Still, I was astounded at the results of our telephone follow-up. Two months after the seminar, Aracelis tracked down all thirty-eight seminar participants. At that time, thirty-five of them, or ninety-three percent, were still maintaining changes in their health behavior! I have never, before or since, heard of such results in secular health education programs.

We witnessed another dramatic example of group change. Pastor Miguel Angel Palomino invited us to his church, mostly out of Latin hospitality. Pastor Miguel's church was among Philadelphia's most vibrant and balanced Hispanic churches, and even outside his denomination, many people viewed him as one of the community's key spiritual leaders. Health was not a priority for him or his church—until the seminar. During the screening he was surprised to find his own blood pressure was perilously elevated, in the range that put him at risk for a stroke. He had never dreamed he had high blood pressure. Both he and I shuddered at what might have happened to him, to his church, and to our community if we had not caught it and gotten him into treatment when we did. For a long time after that, his church maintained an emphasis on the Gospel for the whole person— body, soul, and spirit. Eventually this church led a very effective immunization and evangelism outreach to its neighborhood.

Who would have thought that to keep a church spiritually effective, one must teach its leaders about physical health? Who would have realized that the church that strengthens its neighbors' physical health also strengthens itself spiritually and numerically as a result?

On the other hand, we saw that seminar results seemed to correspond with each church's spiritual and relational vitality. In churches that were not very alive spiritually, our health education had little long-term effect. And in congregations where people simply warmed the pews each Sunday, we were not as effective as in churches where people were actively involved in relationships with one another.

In other words, if you want people to be physically healthy, teach about spiritual and relational health. Years later, this would become a truism in mainstream medical practice. Even the federal government would recognize that churches are often more cost-effective than secular agencies as vehicles for communicating health information and supporting healthy behavior.

◆　◆　◆　◆　◆　◆　◆

Our seminar was a great beginning, but soon we saw a way to extend and increase our results. We could equip people within each church to carry on the vision. Wouldn't it be great to train the follow-up coordinators to think through their group's ongoing health needs? They might be able to plan more creative strategies for continuing health promotion than we ever could. Their churches already trusted them. Certainly they would understand cultural issues that health professionals from a different background would stumble over. Teaching them to teach might be the wisest use of our resources. It would also empower them with self-reliance, which is so scarce in poor communities—and that might stimulate them to do other creative things for themselves.

Even as I spoke to potential donors about this dream of training lay health promoters, I realized I was not the one to carry it out. I had pretty much exhausted all I learned in my week in Evanston. It would be so nice to have a real health educator to do this next phase. Furthermore, I had another job to do. Since Evanston, I had done almost nothing to develop the health center. If we didn't eventually get it going, we would lose credibility with people all over Philadelphia.

I dragged out my notebook from Evanston and began making calls. Yes, the folk at MAP International did know a few health educators scattered around the world who might be between jobs. One tipped me off to Intercristo, a Seattle agency that matches prospective Christian workers with job openings in Christian organizations. Before long I had a dozen or so names of masters' level health educators who spoke Spanish

Over the next few months, Koinonia/Esperanza paid travel expenses for four health educators to come to Philadelphia for interviews. They were all well qualified and fairly impressed with what we were doing—but none accepted the job. I was particularly frustrated with the fourth candidate's trip. She was a delight. Nancy Jo Hoover had consulted on the health effects of a proposed dam in Somalia, developed a sanitation project in a Sudanese refugee camp, worked on medical relief teams in Thailand and Somalia, and trained Afghan refugees in various health programs. Her Spanish was excellent, and she had a real heart for people in desperate need. Furthermore, she liked our community and church. The four-day visit went well until Sunday. During the worship service at our church, she felt she heard God speak to her in her heart, and call her—to Afghanistan!

"God, that's below the belt!" I shouted at the car windows after dropping her off at the airport. "How could you do that to us, and on Esperanza time, yet?"

It didn't seem fair. I had not wanted to be involved in health education in the first place. I had obeyed, as best I knew, and now I was trying to give attention to what God had so clearly let me know was His priority. But He wasn't doing His part. He was even undermining my efforts.

As I pulled the car up through the autumn leaves in front of our house, I caught a glimpse of Him reigning, not only over Esperanza and Philadelphia's health problems, but over the whole world and *all* of its problems. He had created Afghans as well as North Philadelphians. He was concerned about them, too. I saw how I had gradually come to see Him as a servant to my project, rather than me being a servant to His. As King, He had every right to call Nancy Jo to Afghanistan. He could also use Esperanza's money anyway He wanted to. I bowed my head against the steering wheel and quietly asked forgiveness.

That was not the end of the subject. I continued talking to God about getting us a health educator. Clearly, we needed divine help in recruiting one. Three or four weeks later, driving alone down Market Street, I found myself talking out loud.

"Oh God, it was Your idea to get us into this health education business! You know I can't do this and still do the other things You have called me to do! I really need a health educator! If You want us to have health education, You must have someone in mind for the job. Please, please let us find that person!"

Suddenly, I heard an answer, not audibly, but unmistakably in my heart. "I've already heard you. Trust Me."

My prayers changed. I found myself simply affirming God's promise and thanking Him for what He would do. In the next few months I would see Him do other amazing things. But I wouldn't find out for almost a year how wonderfully He would answer this prayer, and why He took that long.

Help From Many Sources

Feeling like a cat with yellow feathers around her mouth, I fastened my seatbelt for the flight to Chicago and tried to keep from grinning. I was on my way to the 1986 autumn board meeting of the Christian Community Health Fellowship. That I should be considered expert enough to be elected to this remarkable group was ludicrous. I would be rubbing shoulders with the "Who's Who" of American providers of Christian health care to the poor—I, who had yet to do anything but talk. Were there that few experts in the world? Or perhaps God had stacked the deck in my favor. I certainly needed more training and contacts to do the job He had given me. Well, I would make the most of it and would learn everything I could.

At dinner that night, I sat across from Len Sharber, the tall, winsome African-American Board President. Len regaled me with fascinating stories. He had moved his family to Austin, on Chicago's west side, a decade or so before so he could do psychotherapy at Circle Health Center. Now its administrator, Len had watched Circle grow into a huge agency. Circle not only provided medical care and counseling in the name of Christ, but also job training, housing rehabilitation, and a variety of other services. Blacks and whites worked together with a brotherhood uncommon even in the Christian world.

Len had arranged for our board to convene at Circle. The next day between sessions, he gave us all a tour. Seeing the impressive facility and meeting some of the warriors who had fought for years to give hope to this community renewed my inspiration. Their God lived in Philly, too.

Each coffee break gave the chance to hear another board member's story. By the end of the weekend, my head was packed with the many methods and models God had used to bring compassionate, spiritually sensitive health care to those who are most overlooked.

Dr. Art Jones, a lanky young blond with an understated manner, particularly impressed me. As a third year medical student, he had founded Lawndale Christian Health Center, now a nationally recognized showpiece for excellence in health care delivery to a poor community. Art and his wife

Linda had moved into the Lawndale neighborhood, one of Chicago's most blighted. Later I discovered how he had influenced the city's politics of health care and health care finance.

To my delight, Art invited me to stay with his family for a few days after the board meeting. Art and Linda shared a duplex with the Wayne Gordons, the young couple who had founded Lawndale Community Church.

Unlocking, then carefully relocking, all three deadlocks on the front door, Art carried my bags up the stairs. We emerged into a simply but attractively furnished apartment. Kelly, their daughter, welcomed me instantly and proudly showed me her school projects. She seemed none the worse for being raised in the inner city. Art and Linda had managed to provide her with a good education even as they identified with their neighbors. They also managed to give me lots of undivided attention, as if my dreams and hopes and goals were really important—and doable.

For a couple of days, I shadowed Art. His days began at the hospital at 6:00 a.m. As one of the few cardiologists in the area, he had to read all the hospital's EKGs of the day before, and then make rounds on the cardiology patients. He had a special personal greeting for nearly everyone. By 8:30 we were at the health center.

The first day a stout middle-aged woman was our initial patient.

"G'morning, Mrs. Jackson! How're you doing? And how are those two young 'uns?"

It wasn't just small talk; Art was really interested in her grand-kids' progress.

"Say, according to this chart, your blood pressure's gone up a little bit. Is the medicine agreeing with you?" While he rechecked her blood pressure himself, Art probed gently how often she might miss taking it, and whether or not its cost was proving prohibitive on her limited income. Then he put down his clipboard and looked up at her.

"Is there stuff going on at home that might be driving your blood pressure up?"

She hesitated, then spoke softly. "Well, I'm worried about my daughter. We haven't heard nothin' from her for four weeks now. Police don't have any clues."

"Oh, I'm so sorry. That's really tough. How're you coping?"

"Well, the ladies at the church been praying for me pretty regularly, and God knows I pray a whole bunch. If it weren't for that, I'd probably go crazy. I'm trying to trust God about this, like the preacher said last week."

"Well, I'll pray for your daughter, too. And how 'bout if we just say a prayer now for you guys?"

"Oh, that'd be great!"

Art bowed his head and briefly lifted Mrs. Jackson, her daughter, and her two grandchildren up to God, asking Him to grant them strength, courage, and help in their time of need. Then he wrote out her prescriptions and wished a better month ahead. As she trotted off to the lab to have her blood drawn, Art turned back to me. "Carolyn, she may seem a little rattled now. But you have no idea how far she has come over the last two years. She's not drinking any more, she's doing a good job of caring for her grandkids, and she's starting to have real friendships with some of the other women in the church here."

Mrs. Jackson was not the only patient that morning with whom Art seemed to have a real relationship. Nor was she the only patient that seemed to be involved with the church on the premises. I heard several in the waiting room talk about going to a church function posted on the bulletin board. I learned that many of the staff also lived in the community and attended the church.

That afternoon, after we ate the sack lunches Linda had packed, Art gave me his own tour of the facility, formerly an abandoned Cadillac dealership. Besides the health center, already overcrowded with six full-time doctors, many volunteer doctors, and support staff, the building housed a lovely worship center and a magnificent gym. The gym was a particular source of pride for Art.

"You see this ceiling?" He pointed to beams which had hung over shiny Cadillacs many years ago. "There was no way this ceiling could be raised. Nor could we get a skiploader in here. The only way to get enough headroom for basketball was to dig the floor out by hand, shovelful by shovelful. Hundreds of kids from the neighborhood hauled all the dirt out of here in wheelbarrows." He grinned. "How's that for sweat equity?"

I grinned back. God help the person who would dare to graffiti those walls!

I pondered the enormous impact of Art and of Wayne Gordon, who had given themselves unreservedly to these neighborhood kids, and of the church they had formed.

Across the street, row houses accommodated a tutoring program and a home renovation project. These projects were staffed by neighborhood people together with suburbanites, many of whom had moved into the neighborhood. A number of homes down the block had a fresh, clean appearance. Art described a couple dozen neighborhood kids who were now in college, and others who were now off drugs and were working. This facility's success was drawing attention. The U.S. government was withdrawing financial support from nearby federally funded health centers and putting it here.

◆ ◆ ◆ ◆ ◆ ◆ ◆

In the evenings we talked. I detected that Art is a brilliant and gifted leader. However, he clearly viewed the projects as the work of the people of the community, particularly those who had become part of Lawndale Christian Church. This was not the first time I had heard of churches spawning spectacular programs which professionals alone could never do. It would not be the last.

I pumped Art and Linda for all the helpful hints they could give. I took pages of notes. I was particularly interested in Art's reference to the Robert Wood Johnson Foundation, which had given start-up funds for their health center.

"How did this start-up grant work?" I asked.

"We had to make up a budget for the first eight years of our operations," Art said. We both laughed. I had trouble making a budget for my household for even a year at a time! Art continued, "Then the Robert Wood Johnson Foundation gave us two dollars for every one dollar we raised for the first five years, and one dollar for every four we raised the last three years. The catch is that our entire share of the money for the whole eight years had to be raised up front. They believe it takes that long for a new health center to stabilize. They don't want to start centers that won't make it." Reasonable enough, I thought.

The prestige of the Robert Wood Johnson matching grant had given Art credibility with a number of Chicago foundations. It didn't hurt that one of the foundation officers arrived the day that Wayne and thirty or forty high-school students had been on top of the building putting on a new roof. She was impressed with that level of community participation. She gave them the money they had requested right away.

"Do you think there is any chance we could get a grant like that?" I pressed.

"Oh, they'd be very interested in you! I'll talk to Terrance Keenan about you. He is our program officer for the Foundation, and he has been really great with us."

I left Chicago in awe of what God had put together there, and excited about what He might do in Philly. I also was grateful for my new mentors.

◆   ◆   ◆   ◆   ◆   ◆   ◆

As 1986 drew to a close, Ted Hewson, now a permanent part of our team, introduced me to a complicated computer spreadsheet he had designed to help us budget—a new concept to me. We spent many evenings poring over it, trying to estimate the cost of each aspect of running a health center. We borrowed figures from Lawndale Christian Health Center and from centers affiliated with other CCHF board members. We tried to guess how many patients would be poor. Some would have federal Medical Assistance, but some would need discounted fees. An eight-year budget would be hard enough to create if we knew what we were doing. For inexperienced amateurs, the task seemed overwhelming. By about March, we had done our best. It appeared we would have to raise $218,000, which the Robert Wood Johnson Foundation would match with another $295,000.

Through the winter I also worked on a formal needs assessment, which Art had said we would need. A community health center had just spent a lot of federal money studying North Philadelphia's health needs, but no one seemed willing to share their study with us. Somewhere I heard of the Freedom of Information Act, which required that information paid for by the government must be available to any person requesting it. How simple, in theory. *Many* phone calls and letters later, I finally received a copy of their study—with a lot of important information blacked out as "proprietary." Yet it was enough, along with the statistics and personal interviews I had already collected, to prove that the area of North Philly we were interested in had vast unmet health needs.

With these two key documents on hand, I called the Robert Wood Johnson Foundation and asked for Terrance Keenan, who had been so helpful to the Lawndale group.

"And what is the purpose of your call?" a secretary inquired.

"I'd like to request an application for the Community Care Funding Partners Program," I responded, as Art had told me to.

"Oh, I'm sorry." The voice was colder this time. "That program closed at the end of 1986."

"But...but Art Jones *said* you would help us," I stuttered, in shock.

The secretary put me on hold. I waited, a cold sweat breaking out on my forehead. Was all of this work for nothing? Had I been laboring only for a pipe-dream?

A new voice came on line. "Are you one of those, those *church*-based health centers, like Dr. Jones's?"

I gulped hard. "Y-yes," I admitted timidly.

"Oh, then we're interested in talking with you!" The Robert Wood Johnson Foundation had apparently come to believe that church-based health care was more cost efficient than secular care. The new voice directed me to send a letter, along with our needs assessment and proposed budget. I was only too happy to comply.

A few weeks later, Dr. Terrance Keenan called me. The Robert Wood Johnson Foundation was willing to re-open this particular funding program for us. When could he come down for a site visit?

We didn't have a site. We had a building we hoped would become a site. Timothy Academy, a Christian elementary school in the neighborhood, had a completely open third floor which they were considering letting us use. There were no walls, plumbing, or electrical wiring in that space, let alone an elevator, which we would need. We had no idea where we might get money to renovate it. But it would have to do. The Lighthouse, a social service agency within view of Timothy Academy, graciously allowed us to use their conference room for the meeting.

Several of us – Ted, my husband Ron, several board members, a fundraising consultant we had hired, and I – gathered at the Lighthouse early in June. Dr. Keenan, a small, balding gentleman, turned out to be not nearly as intimidating as I had imagined. He asked several questions, and then spent quite a bit of time explaining how the matching grant would work. I kept asking, "If you fund us..." He kept answering, "When we fund you...."

The meeting was halfway over before I realized the Robert Wood Johnson Foundation had already decided to give us the grant! I could hardly contain myself. Dr. Keenan finally stood up, warmly shook our hands, and walked out to his car. As soon as the door closed, we shouted and whooped—then joined hands for a fervent prayer of thanksgiving. We were on our way!

None of us dreamed of the major roadblocks we would soon encounter, nor of how dramatically God would turn them around to our benefit.

Above All We Ask or Think

During the next few months I alternately skyrocketed and plummeted on the wildest rollercoaster ride of my life.

Our consultant said donors would be more likely to listen to people actually doing the project than to professional fundraisers. I was certainly no fundraiser. My experience in public speaking and in marketing was limited. I had not even sold Girl Scout cookies very well. Still, no one else on the team had time to seek financial backing. God would have to make me a fundraiser.

That summer the church let me use a computer in the downtown office. I had never operated a computer, and learning to use "Charlie," as I dubbed it, brought to my mind and sometimes to my lips swear words I didn't think I even knew. Eventually, Charlie and I made peace. Scores of donated babysitting hours freed me to invest several weeks in developing a fifty-four page proposal that incorporated all I had learned from our fundraising consultant. Proudly, I sent it to the only two Philadelphia foundations large enough to fund our share of the match.

Then, completely drained, I escaped for a couple of weeks with Ron, Melody and David to a primitive cabin in the back woods of Maine. It would be good to get to know my husband and kids again.

For the first several days, I did little but sleep and fish. Later, while trying to think and pray, I recalled tales of busy, productive people who had abruptly dropped out of everything and spent the next ten years watching television. Suddenly I understood their reaction. I, too, was dangerously close to burnout. I began to see I was not strong enough to bring Esperanza Health Center into being. Either God would do it, or it would not happen. I left Maine rested, but with a renewed sense of my finiteness. Given my family responsibilities, I realized I could work twenty hours a week on Esperanza, but no more.

◆　◆　◆　◆　◆　◆　◆

A week or two after we got home, one foundation returned the proposal with a routine "We are sorry to inform you...." The other took a little longer. Since one of our board members was a trustee of that foundation, we thought we would be well received. The last week of September, though, we received a polite rejection notice. A private, rather cold letter to our trustee board member detailed several reasons why we were not worth funding. He was outraged. He called everyone he knew, throwing the considerable weight of his influence into the process—without success. I was crushed.

Over the next couple of weeks my disappointment grew into depression. I had exhausted myself all summer—for nothing. Where else could we even begin to look for the $218,000 we needed to get the Robert Wood Johnson grant? For the second time I asked myself, *Was this all a wild goose chase?*

October brought the first of two fall retreats for our church leaders. The crisp air and extravagantly colored foliage of Spruce Lake revived my spirits a little. Rappelling down the mountainside with dear friends reminded me of the importance of trust and laughter. Later, when we met in small groups to pray, I was ready to open my heart. I shared my confusion about what seemed so clearly to have been God's leading, and my discouragement over the rejection letters. Gently, firmly, my friends lifted me to the Father. Slowly some peace seeped into my heart.

I was looking forward to the second leadership retreat scheduled to take place at an equally beautiful site the weekend before Thanksgiving. Early in November, however, a letter arrived from Covenant Fellowship, a new church in Philadelphia's suburbs. Could I speak to the congregation for ten minutes on the Sunday of the retreat? I quickly called the pastor, grateful for the invitation but wondering if another date would do. No, it wouldn't. This was to be the church's first specific focus on the needs of the poor, and he wanted to tie it to Thanksgiving.

A bit miffed that I would miss some of the retreat, I slipped some church clothes into our suitcase next to my jeans. Throughout the retreat, I found myself distracted, wondering what would happen Sunday morning. I had never given a talk like this before. I woke up early Sunday and tried to quiet my heart before God, still not sure what I should say. While everyone else filed down to breakfast, I slipped into the parking lot and began the hour-long drive to Covenant Fellowship. As I drove, I sensed a quiet Presence lifting me, strengthening me.

I walked in a couple of minutes after the worship had started. The Presence I had felt in the car was stronger here. Most people were already engrossed in worship of a God who has unparalleled compassion for the earth's poor and afflicted. Each song pointed to His profound identification with those who suffer, or His strong arm stretched out on their behalf. A young woman read from the Psalms:

> *"But you, O God, do see trouble and grief;*
> *you consider it to take it in hand.*
> *The victim commits himself to you;*
> *you are the helper of the fatherless."*[32]

Everywhere, I saw faces turned upward with tear-stained cheeks crinkled in smiles, eyes closed. I gathered that many were remembering God's help in personal times of distress.

After about forty-five minutes, Rev. Bill Patton stood to preach. Bill was young; yet in only three years he had drawn together this congregation of about five hundred. He preached simply but powerfully about God's concern for the poor and His expectation that we share His concern. Then, he called me forward.

The Presence I had felt all morning enveloped me. I found myself speaking clearly and passionately about a community in North Philadelphia with needs almost unimaginable to most suburbanites. I spoke about the God who wants those living in that community to receive healing for body, soul, spirit, and neighborhood – and about our opportunity to help deliver that healing. Then I sat down for the offering and benediction.

As soon as the congregation was dismissed, I was besieged. For the next hour, one person after another pressed his or her business card on me.

"I'm a real estate agent," shared a Center City businessman. "Perhaps I could host a luncheon for my business associates, where you could talk about this." (He did; over $3,000 came in at that luncheon.)

"I'm a business executive," interjected a middle-aged woman. "Perhaps I could help in some way. (She did; her advice on setting up procedures proved most helpful.)

---

[32] Psalm 10:14

A tall, burly youth waited patiently. "I'm just a college student. I don't have any money, but my buddies and I could stuff the envelopes for your fundraising letters!" (They did—for the next three or four years.)

When the crowd finally dispersed, I began packing my brochures and pictures. As I shoved the last one into my box, Bill handed me an envelope containing the morning's offering. I thanked him, carried my stuff to the car, and settled into the driver's seat. I slipped the keys into the ignition, then opened the envelope. The check was written for $12,454!

As I pulled onto the highway, the Presence began to speak—not audibly, but unmistakably—in my heart. "Don't you see, Carolyn? I'm God! I own the cattle on a thousand hills! I don't need big Philadelphia foundations! If I choose to fund this entire Robert Wood Johnson match with ten- and twenty-dollar gifts from My people, I can do that. This is My project! I am in charge! Now you be quiet, do your homework, and watch Me work!"

"Yes, Sir!" I sang all the way back to the retreat.

◆ ◆ ◆ ◆ ◆ ◆ ◆

During December and January we saw God's activity on several fronts.

Terry Monaco, an art teacher from our church, had assigned her graphic design students the task of creating a logo, letterhead, brochure, and business card for a newly developing health center in North Philadelphia. On the due date, I went into class and viewed twenty-three excellent presentations. Terry and I picked the best, modified them slightly, and prepared them for printing. That saved us the expense of hiring a professional designer.

Meanwhile, another group from our church began working on a fundraising slide show. Ron came up with the basic idea. Someone talked a professional writer into producing a wonderful script. Ramona Doyle, a gifted artist on our church's North Philly evangelism team, developed a storyboard. She also found appropriate background music and got the publishers' permissions to use it. David Gentry, a professional photographer, wandered through good and bad sections of Philly, capturing contrasting street scenes and poignant people shots. Dan Moser, a graduate student with a rich bass voice, agreed to narrate the show. Several talented musicians and techs mixed a top-notch sound track. Terry added graphics. Over the next few months, a professional-quality slide show emerged. It captivated audiences across the country, persuading hundreds of people to join the fight for true health and wholeness in North Philadelphia. The whole production cost less than $500.

I thanked God that others were picking up responsibility for Esperanza. The twenty-hour-a-week limit seemed to be binding. Sometimes I would finish my twenty hours by Wednesday evening. If I spent even an additional hour on Esperanza on Thursday or Friday, something bad would happen. Four-year-old David would start misbehaving. Melody would have trouble at school. Ron and I would start arguing over trivia. Or I would get the flu. God seemed to be keeping me on a short leash. Maybe He really cared about my physical and emotional health as much as He did about Esperanza. Why was that so hard for me to believe? Maybe He also wanted me to trust Him, as I had never trusted before. Maybe He wanted me to experience, first hand, His trustworthiness.

Just before Christmas, I got an unsolicited call from Van Weigel, director of the MBA program in economic development at Eastern College. He was seeking internship placements for graduate students and had heard about Esperanza. Could we possibly use help four days a week from an MBA student? He had one young woman in mind. She had studied Spanish and hoped eventually to become a missionary to Mexico. And, oh yes, World Vision had provided a grant to cover three quarters of her salary!

Pretty, petite Karen DeHaven more than made up the extra hours I was not "allowed" to work. She knew a lot more than I did about accounting, marketing, databases and other aspects of business. She brought order to much of my chaos. She quickly grasped the spiritual implications of what we were doing, and her fervent prayers bolstered my own faith. Before long, she announced that, after her three month internship, she would continue working with us at her present minimal salary until Esperanza was up and running and she could find and train a replacement. Neither of us dreamed she would stay for four years as our business manager, let alone move into the Latino community in order to identify more fully with the people we served. Gradually I saw that in Karen God had brought me not only a co-worker, but a friend. Those four years were to subject us to stresses we could in no way have imagined. When my own vision clouded, Karen's loyalty and love became signposts pointing me to God.

In late January 1988, Karen took a phone call from another health center across town. "The program officer from the Public Welfare Foundation is going to visit us this afternoon," she heard. "Would you like an hour with her?"

Without even having written them a letter? Would we ever! Quickly I made arrangements for a couple of board members to meet Karen and me at Timothy Academy. The program officer joined us there at three o'clock. We gave her a tour of the empty third floor, showed her our architectural drawings, then sat down in the school library to share our dreams and discuss the Robert Wood Johnson commitment. She listened attentively.

"Yes, I think you have something here. You should definitely submit a proposal to us."

"How much do you think we should ask for?" I queried.

"Well, somewhere between $40,000 and $60,000, I would think."

I had planned to ask only for $25,000. They granted our proposal for $50,000!

◆　◆　◆　◆　◆　◆　◆

Before this grant came through we experienced two major setbacks.

Early in March, in the morning mail, Ron found a thin envelope from the Robert Wood Johnson Foundation. He read it, then silently sent it upstairs with Karen to me. The Foundation was sorry to inform us that, since they had not heard from us for nine months, they were canceling our matching grant.

I sank into my desk chair. I could hardly breathe. I glanced at the boxes of bright yellow and blue glossy brochures stacked in the corner of our attic office, just back from the printer. On the shelf above them were the carousels and tapes of our new slide show, ready for booking. Speechless, I handed the letter to Karen. She scanned it, then together we trotted downstairs to find Ron. Quietly, while tears streamed down my face, the three of us laid the matter before God.

We went back upstairs and began making calls. I phoned Art Jones, who agreed to talk to the Robert Wood Johnson Foundation on our behalf. We spoke to every person of influence we could think of. We asked everyone we knew to pray.

The next days were among the blackest of my life. Without the Robert Wood Johnson grant, we had no credibility with the public. If the grant were dead, so were all of our brochures and our slide show. If the grant were really dead, so was Esperanza. When they heard about the letter, some of our supporters were ready to play the funeral dirge.

What about Your promises, God?

I waited. I fasted. I had thought fasting was for "spiritual" concerns; this was "just" a social action project. Could prayer and fasting be as necessary for successful social action as for a more overtly spiritual enterprise?

I reviewed how this whole project started, almost on its own. I pondered the distinct word that had grown in my heart on the way home from Covenant Fellowship. I recalled the resources that came together so amazingly over the last few months. Slowly a conviction crystallized. Esperanza was God's idea from the beginning – not ours. He had started the process; He would finish it. I could not even claim credit for this faith. It had been bestowed as a gift.

A couple of weeks passed. Based on the number of calls to his office, Dr. Keenan became convinced that a good number of people were committed to seeing Esperanza materialize. He became our advocate to the Foundation's president and vice president. They, in turn, took the matter to the trustees. At the end of March, we received another letter. The grant would be reinstated, *if* we could raise our entire share of the match by the end of December.

◆　◆　◆　◆　◆　◆　◆

Although we didn't realize it, we had just been handed a magic formula for fundraising: a large matching grant and a deadline. I began getting invitations to speak at churches throughout the greater Philadelphia area, and even in California. The Christian Broadcasting Network flew me to Florida to be interviewed on one of their talk shows. John Perkins came to Philadelphia to speak at a fundraising banquet catered by a local woman's missionary group.

Checks began coming from as far away as Alaska. Corporations gave. Individuals sent pledges. Some of the most generous people were barely off welfare. A college student, poor at the time, figured that in three years he would have a good job, and promised to give $2,500 a year for four years. A foundation to which I had never even sent a letter gave an unsolicited $10,000. Another non-profit organization gave $5,000 of its own hard-won income. In September, two foundations separately asked how much we needed to complete the match. *Each* gave the $30,000 remaining.

That was helpful, because as Karen and I reviewed the budget, we found item after item costing more than we had anticipated. We also realized that a computer system, not originally included, would be indispensable. We worked up a revised budget which we hoped would be more realistic—but it would require an extra $260,000. We would have to raise an additional $130,000, and we would need the foundation to match it.

Nervously, we called the Robert Wood Johnson Foundation. Graciously, they agreed to match whatever sum we could raise by December 31. Karen and I hung up the phone and started giggling. After all, an additional $130,000 was no more impossible than the original $218,000 had been.

By Thanksgiving we had $218,000 on hand. We grinned and kept working. And praying. We laid aside Esperanza business and spent Christmas and New Years' with our families. On January 2, 1989, we climbed the stairs to the office and totaled what had come in. In addition to the entire original match amount, we had received another $131,000! Together with the Robert Wood Johnson money, that would amount to well over a half million dollars.

What a party we had a few weeks later! Dr. Keenan, representing the Robert Wood Johnson Foundation, attended, along with several other major donors. We invited everyone who had contributed time, sweat, or talent. The crowd included people from at least thirty different professions—besides health professionals. The two hundred guests were from all races and classes. We chatted shyly, nibbled hors d'oeuvres, and drank in the unity flowing in that room. We acknowledged each person's contribution, watched the slide show one last time, and basked in the rich tones of "To God Be the Glory" from a gospel soloist. Even the non-religious joined in singing "Great is Thy Faithfulness."

◆　◆　◆　◆　◆　◆　◆

The Robert Wood Johnson match was not our only miracle that year. The second setback, which also occurred the previous March, ultimately proved to be a gift as well. Just after the grant-canceling letter arrived, an inspector discovered asbestos in the Timothy Academy building. In the space allocated to us, the asbestos was confined to floor and ceiling tiles. A few workers could have taken out those tiles over a weekend, but that would have been illegal, and possibly dangerous as well. We were told not to worry; a professional asbestos removal company would let us know within two weeks how much proper removal would cost. It would likely be affordable. Then, we could start renovations.

We waited two weeks. Without explaining why, the company said it would be another two weeks. The same was true at the end of those two weeks, and the next two, and the next two.

June came. A team of volunteer construction workers from Chicago arrived. We could not use them due to the asbestos situation. We sent them to Habitat for Humanity, which was happy to accept their services.

July and August slipped by. Our volunteer architect from Helps International Ministries had to go on to another project, along with his group of volunteer construction professionals. I could see our construction costs spiraling. We had hoped to do the renovations, including installation of an elevator, for about $150,000. Now it was looking more like $225,000 or $250,000. I had no idea where we'd get the money. The Robert Wood Johnson grant was NOT for building renovations.

September pulled in. Bonnie, our administrator, had visited all forty-two alternative locations in North Philadelphia. Not a single one was both suitable and available. Still there was no word from the asbestos removal company. By the end of September I was frantic. The Robert Wood Johnson site visit was scheduled for October 11, and we didn't have a site. Furthermore, we couldn't possibly put together a final budget without financial information on a legitimate location. The December deadline was non-negotiable. I found myself yelling wildly at Ron, "Do you know, we have to have a site within a week?" And he yelled back, "Do you know that's impossible?"

The first day of October, Bonnie heard that a Catholic social service agency right in the center of the Latino community had given six-months' notice to their landlord. For as many as thirty years, Casa del Carmen had been well known to the community. At one time they had housed a medical clinic. Three of their offices already had sinks. Now they were moving to a convent where they would have free rent.

That afternoon, Bonnie and I and our architect walked through the facility. We were astounded by how few changes would have to be made to serve our purposes. We called an emergency board meeting at Casa del Carmen a couple of evenings later. At first the board balked, because there was more room than we could initially use or afford. Indeed, who would want to sublet second floor space in that neighborhood? The next afternoon I found six non-profit organizations who expressed interest in subletting space. On the strength of that interest, the board approved the site in a conference call. I didn't even care that all six organizations backed out within the week. We would deal with that later. Esperanza had a new home, in an ideal location—just in time!

◆ ◆ ◆ ◆ ◆ ◆ ◆

Six months later, when Casa del Carmen left, we started to work. A professional designer gave us a beautiful layout and color scheme. Ron acted as general contractor. A carpenter from Alaska got his church to donate plane fare to fly him to Philly. He gave his vacation to supervise the major structural alterations. While volunteers worked with him, Ron, Karen, and I scrounged equipment from medical schools, hospitals, retiring doctors, missionary agencies, and auctions. A corporation gave us money for brand new, top-of-the-line medical equipment from my remaining wish list. Ten weeks and forty-five volunteers later, the site was ready for occupancy. Total renovation cost amounted to about $12,000, as compared to the $150,000 we had expected to spend at Timothy Academy!

While the renovations proceeded, several other surprising things fell into place.

Rev. Billy Robinson, an experienced psychotherapist, offered to counsel our patients, for only whatever fees he could collect. I had no idea we could get counseling on board so soon.

Dr. Bill Kussmaul, a cardiologist, committed to volunteer time each week, as did Dr. Phil Siu, a pediatrician. Their care would supplement the care that Dr. Mike Moore, our full-time family physician, and I would provide. Their commitments would last for many years.

Dr. Eliezer Martinez, a Puerto Rican psychologist and minister, offered to train community members for peer counseling. This began the fulfillment of one of my long-term dreams. We started planning a course to begin in July.

Finally, four weeks before opening day, Coral Andino, a Puerto Rican nurse with a master's degree and a good job in psychiatric nursing, committed her life to Christ in our kitchen. She burst in for our lunch together the next week, asking if she could quit her job and work at Esperanza, in whatever capacity we would designate. I had already seen her proposals for community health education. I knew her to be warm, outgoing, passionately concerned for her people, and sensitive to nuances of Puerto Rican culture, as I could never be. Coral became our first paid staff member, a full-time health educator.

Thus it came about that on June 15, 1989, Esperanza Health Center opened, a far bigger and better health center than any of us had imagined. None of us had envisioned the whole picture. It left no doubt in our minds as to Who had put Esperanza together. *"To Him who is able to do immeasurably more than all we ask or imagine, according to His power that is at work within us, to Him be glory...."*[33]

Life on Fifth Street

Tired but exhilarated, I pulled out the vacuum cleaner. By any standards, the party had been a great success. The Puerto Rican band we hired sight unseen turned out to be excellent. Our congressman showed up to cut the big blue ribbon across the door. Lots of folk from the community, as well as from churches and city agencies, came to cheer and tour and savor Puerto Rican goodies. Ted's camera caught Ron giving me a congratulatory kiss under the balloons around the front desk. The whole day seemed almost surreal: a seven-and-a-half-year dream suddenly popped into reality.

Now we needed to prepare for patients. While I vacuumed, Karen finished testing our new computer system. She had set it up so patients without insurance could be seen at discounted rates according to their income. Even if we could have afforded it, we knew it would mar people's dignity if we treated them for free. But we also knew most people in our neighborhood could not afford the rates charged by hospital doctors. We would later find that only 6% of our patients could pay full fees.

Migdalia DeJesus, a young mother from the community, prepared clipboards at the front desk. Migdalia had not worked in a health center before, but her quick learning, her love for people, and her view of this job as ministry assured us that we had made the right choice for our first receptionist.

The next morning Karen, Migdalia, Coral, and I gathered in the nurse's office to pray together. This was to become a staff tradition that would last at least seventeen years. We thanked God for all He had done for us, and we prayed for the patients who would soon come. We asked for divine help to respond to their needs as Jesus would.

That first day we saw only four patients, but they provided a portrait of those who would follow. One was homeless and mentally ill. The second had complicated family problems. The other two spoke no English.

I begged God for help with my Spanish. We had to be able to communicate well in a Latino context. A few months before, while Ron and Melody were out of town, David and I had stayed with a Puerto Rican family. Beba Seguinot, my hostess, had kindly but relentlessly grilled me whenever she thought I was just pretending to understand. I had learned more in those nine days than in a whole semester of college Spanish. More recently, Coral had stayed up till 3:00 a.m. helping me translate a sermon when I was invited to speak in a Spanish church. Then a week or two before we opened, the staff had prayed me through a couple of call-in radio talk shows in Spanish. What a way to learn! But as I had seen so often, God does not call anyone to a task without providing the ability to perform it.

I also prayed for help with my clinical skills. I was a little scared. I had not done clinical medicine since before David was born, almost six years before. I had studied hard and passed an Advanced Achievement in Internal Medicine exam a couple of years back, but that did not fill me with confidence. A new disease named AIDS had entered our community since I last practiced. How dared we advertise ourselves as a Christian health center if we offered anything other than really competent medical care?

◆　◆　◆　◆　◆　◆　◆

Both Bill Kussmaul and Phil Siu came in that first week. Their presence meant we could be a multi-specialty group practice right from the beginning. Where else in North Philly could our patients get affordable yet top-notch specialty care in cardiology and pediatrics? Furthermore, if I had questions about an electrocardiogram or a sick kid when Bill and Phil were not there, I could just pick up the phone and call.

Still, I couldn't wait for Mike to get back from vacation. As a family physician, he would complement my skills in a way that a specialist never could. He and Pam were spending a few days away before plunging into work at Esperanza. During the two years they had lived in the *barrio*, they had learned more than they could have imagined about the needs of their neighbors. They knew the risks of letting their baby play on the sidewalk in front of their house and the annoyance of having to chase drug dealers off their porch at midnight. I was glad they could get away. But I really looked forward to the end of those two weeks.

Mike quickly proved to be an incredible partner. I learned to lean heavily on him whenever I considered treatment options for a patient. I also admired the way he tapped into deep wells of compassion for his patients, even when unpleasant situations surfaced at the end of long days.

With two toddlers at home, Pam decided to work at the health center only one day a week. However, she organized a cadre of volunteer nurses to work on a regular basis. She also established procedures and quality control measures. I thanked God for her organizational gifts as well as her nursing skills.

Foreseeing the need to learn Spanish, Mike and Pam had spent three months at the Instituto Lenguaje in Costa Rica. They were the first of several Esperanza doctors to go at their own expense to Central America to learn Spanish via "immersion." I was always surprised at how much each could learn in 8-12 weeks. Mike didn't quite get all the grammar down while he was there, and now he was a little rusty. But he worked without a translator from day one. Soon his patients were pouring their hearts out to him as they never could have done in English.

The week that Mike got back, I received a letter from Intercristo, a computer-matching employment service for Christian organizations worldwide. The letter said a recent Wheaton College graduate in sociology was looking for a job where she could use her Spanish. Marialena Gant, a diminutive red-head with an infectious laugh, visited Esperanza a couple of weeks later. I took her to lunch at a small Puerto Rican restaurant down the street. I ordered "chuchifritos," not realizing that I would be getting pigs' ears. I managed to get a few bites down, but I miserably failed this test of Puertorican-ness. Marialena, who had grown up in Argentina with missionary parents, had no such difficulties. Her Spanish was flawless, and she instantly fit into our community.

I explained to Marialena that though we had not budgeted for a social worker in the Robert Wood Johnson grant, we certainly could use one. We did have enough money to pay a social worker's salary for one month, and we had applied for a grant to pick up the salary thereafter. Would she consider coming under those circumstances?

Crazy lady—she moved a thousand miles, found an apartment in the *barrio*, and reported for work. We found immediately she was an invaluable team member. She had a unique gift for drawing us together—partly through the graffiti board she posted in the back hallway, partly through her zany sense of humor and propensity to celebrate at the least excuse, partly through her perspective born of years of international exposure. We frequently found signs on the refrigerator announcing "NOTHING IS THE END OF THE WORLD EXCEPT THE END OF THE WORLD!" or other such gems.

◆ ◆ ◆ ◆ ◆ ◆ ◆

She also became indispensable in dealing with patients.

We had already found that our patients were more difficult to care for than those in the usual suburban practice. They were sicker, with more than twice the diabetes and hypertension of the Caucasian population. Furthermore, their control of chronic illnesses was poorer. They could not afford the food needed for special low-cholesterol or weight-loss diets, and they had trouble finding safe places for exercise. They often delayed coming for medical care because of its cost, so they experienced more complications, such as blindness and stroke. Add to that mix high-risk pregnancies and complications of sexually transmitted diseases and drug abuse, and the challenges of inner-city medicine towered before us.

However, these medical problems were often inextricably entwined with non-medical problems that drastically affected their outcomes.

Housing was a big issue. How could I help Nilsa, the 9-year-old girl who came in after a rat bit her in her bedroom at 3 a.m.? Was I supposed to just bandage her finger? Her mom showed me photos of huge holes in her baseboards, which her landlord refused to fix. Or how could I help Jose, a homeless schizophrenic man with active tuberculosis? Every time he was hospitalized, he was discharged to a shelter as soon as he was no longer contagious—but long before he was cured. He was afraid to stay in the shelter because he had been beaten up there before. Within a day he would be back on the streets, where no one could make sure he took his medicine. This off-and-on treatment was guaranteed to produce drug resistant germs. A few weeks later, he would be back at Esperanza, coughing at our receptionist. After a while, I conducted all of our office visits on the sidewalk in front of the health center so as not to risk giving drug-resistant TB to our staff.

Education was another factor. Vilma, now 45 years old, was a juvenile diabetic who never learned to read because her diabetes kept her out of school so much. She faithfully checked her blood sugar four times daily, yet her control was terrible because she could not read food labels. She already had endured her first bypass surgery and amputation of one leg. In our community, where only 30% of adults had graduated from high school, she was far from alone. On the other hand, Kevin *had* just graduated from high school a year ago. When I handed him a set of instructions, I was shocked to hear his brother explain that he could not read. What was with our school system?

And where were the decent jobs? Miguel's horrible skin rash was a contact allergy related to chemicals he used at work, but his family could not afford for him to be unemployed. Tina's physical symptoms were clearly related to sleep deprivation, but at minimum wage she had to work two full-time jobs to provide for her children. I learned that full time work at minimum wage for a mother with three kids provides a salary 25% *below* the federal poverty level.

Family issues complicated health problems. I worked with Luis for months on his diabetes. At length we concluded that his worry over his son's drug abuse was what was driving up his blood sugar. Virginia needed blood pressure medicine from our sample closet every month because she couldn't afford to buy it. However, many months she couldn't come to get it because she could not find someone to stay for an hour or two with her husband, who had Alzheimer's. Bonita, in her late fifties, had suddenly inherited the responsibility of caring for three grandchildren when their crack-addicted mother walked out. Diagnosing her backaches as stress-related was easy, but how could we help?

Immigration problems took their toll. Maria was a newborn with congenital defects requiring surgery. Born here, she was an American citizen eligible for Medicaid. However, her parents were afraid to apply because they were illegal aliens and feared deportation. I was pretty sure Martina's terrible headaches were related to the report she just received that her daughter, still in El Salvador with relatives, had been running off with the "bad" boy who lives down the street, and no one was doing anything about it. She could not bring her daughter to the States, but she would jeopardize all possibilities of a brighter future for her other children if she returned home.

Worst of all, violence inserted itself into nearly everyone's story. Almost everybody I met, clinic staff as well as patients, had a relative or friend who had been attacked, if not killed. Denise struggled for years to overcome the emotional legacy of abuse she suffered in childhood. Just as she seemed to be approaching physical and mental stability, her 16-year-old son was mowed down on his block in a drive-by shooting. If her asthma and blood pressure were difficult to control before, how would we help her now? I also remembered Vivian, who adamantly refused to go to the hospital for tests. She insisted that her ex-boyfriend's cronies who haunted that area would rape her. A bit to my surprise, her fears proved valid, though the rape occurred a little distance from the hospital.

So Marialena had her job cut out for her. Unfortunately, the grant to pay her salary did not come through. We could only pay her half-time—not enough for her to live on. It didn't take long for her to find a half dozen job offers from other agencies eager to get their hands on a bilingual social worker. But they all wanted her full-time. Marialena wasn't sure she wanted to leave Esperanza altogether.

A few weeks into her stay in Philadelphia an incident helped her decide. Mike called her to help with a 10-year-old whose behavior, according to his mom, was completely out of control. They learned that Henry worked as a "runner," delivering cocaine for drug lords who ruled his corner. His bosses had apparently introduced Henry to more than easy money and chemical highs. Early in Mike's and Marialena's session with Henry he described his involvement in occult practices. A bit later he began shrieking about demons coming to get him. Mike and Marialena stayed with him for five hours—restraining, praying, confronting, comforting, talking, praying again—before Henry found peace. Afterwards, a pale and somewhat disheveled Marialena burst into my office and plopped herself in the chair beside my desk.

"How'd it go?" I asked. It had been difficult to think about anything else during the struggle in the room down the hallway. I had been praying under my breath, as had most of the staff.

"He's wiped out," she replied. "But he's now talking rationally. We're going to try to get him into a home for boys outside of the city. But Carolyn, what if we had not had the Lord? What hope would there be for a kid like that?"

The next morning she came into my office even before she took off her jacket. "Carolyn, I was thinking all last night, what if I were working for a secular agency, where I couldn't pray for clients? What in the world could I do for all of the Henrys out there? That would be a sure formula for burn out! Money or no money, I'm not leaving Esperanza!"

She was as good as her word. For a while she worked the other half-time with us as receptionist, while Migdalia left to have her baby. When we hired a full-time receptionist, I trained Marialena as a medical assistant. She picked up on the history- and blood-pressure-taking skills quickly, but she made creatively awful faces when I insisted she learn to draw blood from me. We gave it our best shot on two or three occasions. Finally we decided she would be a great medical assistant even without blood drawing skills. Gradually she also began picking up housecleaning jobs to subsidize her Esperanza salary. The following year we found a way to bring her on full time.

* * * * * * *

The principle Marialena discovered with Henry began surfacing in many encounters with patients. Even the best of care for patients' physical, emotional, and social needs was often not enough.

A couple of months after the clinic opened, Myra came to see me for severe stomach pains. I gave her the usual ulcer treatments, to which she responded only briefly. It soon came out that her relationship with her boyfriend, her four-year-old's father, carried tremendous tension. I convinced them to see Dr. Martinez for counseling in their own language. Still, several weeks into the counseling Myra was back with stomach pains worse than ever. I mustered my nerve and asked her, "Myra, do you believe God knows and cares about what you are going through?" She started crying and poured out a tale of confusion and guilt and resentment about how some Christians had let her down. Little by little she was able to focus on the God of the Bible, who *had* been with her, whether she had made good choices or bad, and who loved her enough to make it possible for her to be cleansed and reconciled to Him. A few minutes later I led her in a simple prayer of repentance and faith. When we finished, she looked at me, beaming. "*Muchisimas gracias!* I feel so much better now!"

It was three years before I saw Myra again. She had just had an emergency appendectomy (unrelated to her previous ulcer disease), and she decided to come to Esperanza to have her stitches taken out. While I snipped, she thanked me for the prayer years before and for the difference it made in her life. She had gotten into a church, broken off the relationship with her previous boyfriend, and obtained a better job. She was engaged to a wonderful Christian man without her previous boyfriend's habits. And she had no further stomach pains.

Joanna came in with insomnia and poor appetite. It didn't take long to understand why she was depressed. Abandoned by her husband, without other family in the area, alienated from her church, she was raising two small children completely alone. I tried to communicate my concern for her, and I shared God's love for her briefly in the exam room. Then I directed her to the lab to have some blood drawn. While I saw my next patient, our lab tech, Ada, took over where I had left off. Soon Joanna was asking Ada questions about God she had been carrying around for years. Before she left, she and Ada prayed, asking God to come into her life in a new way. Ada arranged to pick her up for church on Sunday. The next time I saw her, she was feeling much better.

A bit later, Christine and her mom came to see me. Christine's severe kidney infection was diagnosed in the emergency room a few days before. Though her fever had abated and her vomiting stopped, her mom was quite concerned that her back pain was not yet better. I examined Christine, then left her mom in the exam room while I walked her down to the lab for a urine specimen. On the way, I asked about risk factors for urinary tract infections.

"Are you sexually active?"

After a long pause, she replied, "No."

"Have you been sexually active in the past?" I probed gently.

After a longer pause, "Yes." Christine's face had turned slightly red.

"How recently?"

"About a week ago."

I explained briefly how the mild trauma of infrequent sexual activity can predispose a woman to bladder infections which can lead to kidney infections. I gave her a container for a urine specimen. Ada was busy, so I offered her a seat near the lab and began processing the urine myself. The results showed the antibiotics were working. I sat down next to her to explain that she should be better within a couple of days. She responded with a weak smile. I realized there was more to the story than I knew so far. Noticing the sparkling diamond on her left hand, I asked,

"When are you getting married?"

"Next April."

"How do you feel about having sex before you are married?"

"Terrible."

"Tell me about it."

"My boyfriend and I are both members of the First Baptist Church. We've been at Bible school. We both know it is wrong."

"But you're trapped?"

"Yeah. Big time."

"Can you move your wedding date up?"

"We already moved it up from June. My mom is planning a big wedding, and I don't think she would be willing to move it up any more."

"Christine, you need help. When you and your boyfriend are doing something you deeply believe to be wrong, you are laying a poor foundation for a marriage. Is there someone in your church that you trust, other than your parents, to whom you could really talk about this?"

She was silent for a moment. 'Yes, there is."

"Then you need to go and talk to that person, and let him or her walk you and your boyfriend through the process of repentance and reconciliation with God. Maybe you can work out some practical steps to avoid falling in the future. Maybe it would help you and your boyfriend if you had someone to be accountable to. And maybe, if you all think it is wise, that person could go with you, as your advocate, to talk to your parents about moving up the wedding date."

Christine dabbed her eyes with a Kleenex and smiled more broadly. "That sounds really good. I think we can do that."

On the way back to the exam room, I discovered Christine also took bubble baths, the other major risk factor for urinary tract infections. To her mom I said, "The urine test shows the infection is responding to antibiotics. Christine should be better in a couple of days. Furthermore, we discovered she has been putting herself at risk for urinary tract infections by taking bubble baths. If she stops doing that, or anything else that might put her at risk, she should be fine in the future."

On her way out, Christine's mom made some disparaging remarks about the money wasted on Christine's diamond. She had settled for a plain wedding band; why couldn't her daughter? I realized that Christine might not encounter much empathy from her mother about larger issues. Nonetheless, the grateful look from Christine as we shook hands gave me hope that she would find access to the support she would need to make good decisions.

So what was this? This young lady had opened up to me about spiritual matters she would not have discussed with her pastor. And she was not the only one. Day after day I found perfect strangers telling me things they had never told anyone. Of course, my white coat gave me the right to ask questions no one else would dare to ask. But it was amazing to see how eager my patients were to talk about spiritual subjects with someone who would not condemn them but would help them reconnect with God. We at Esperanza, it seemed, functioned as secular priests.

It wasn't until years later that I found hundreds of scientific papers documenting the benefits of wholesome religion on physical and mental health and the improved healing in patients whose doctors offer spiritual help in addition to medical help. All I knew at this time was that an awful lot of our patients really wanted to talk about spiritual issues, and the spiritual issues often had profound connections to their physical problems.

From a medical standpoint, physical health seemed to require spiritual care.

From a spiritual viewpoint, "the fields were ripe for harvest." My husband, a pastor, didn't have half the opportunities I had every day to touch people spiritually. Where in the world could I be better positioned to help people connect with God at the point of their needs?

Who's in Charge Here?

"Three-and-a-half-year-old Vincent is no longer trying to stab people in his play as a result of counseling he and his family have received at Esperanza."

That seemed like a good opener for our newsletter, inviting all of our friends and associates to Esperanza's first birthday party. Billy had just outlined Vincent's tragic story to me in the hallway. Mike, Phil, Marialena, and Coral had presented me with a half dozen other patient vignettes to use. I enjoyed writing newsletters, sharing such poignant stories. But writing was just one item of the endless stack of administrative duties facing me. I thought I would never find the surface of my desk.

While I was thinking about the next paragraph, Karen tossed an envelope on top of my papers. "Take a look at that!"

The letter, addressed to a Christian counseling center in the suburbs, had my name scrawled across the bottom. The author, a David J. Willoughby, had just finished a Master's degree in counseling and was looking for a job. The center paragraph drew my attention:

"I grew up in Colombia, South America, and would like to use my knowledge of Spanish and the Latin culture to help minister to people of other cultural backgrounds."

Certainly, we could use more help with counseling. Billy was swamped, and we managed to keep a couple of volunteer counselors busy, also. But we had no budget for counseling. Billy was living only on what his patients were able to give him directly, and he was barely making ends meet.

I called Mr. Willoughby, mostly out of politeness. He was fascinated by my description of Esperanza. Despite my bleak predictions about salaried job opportunities, he wanted to fly in from Virginia to visit.

A week later, a tall well-built man in his mid-thirties walked into our waiting room. His blond hair, slightly curly and thinning a bit on top, swept back from a strong forehead. His blue eyes met and held mine as he firmly shook my hand.

After a tour of the health center, we sat down in my office to chat. The son of missionaries, David had spent his first 15 years in Colombia. After returning to the States and finishing college, he worked in administration of a small college—for two years he actually was Vice President. Then the college folded for lack of money, and David had the agonizing task of closing down its affairs. Two years later, with his new Master's degree, he was ready for another challenge.

I was too swamped to take him to lunch. He assured me he didn't mind; sampling some of the street vendors' Hispanic foods would rekindle pleasant memories for him.

Four hours later, he returned, looking like a rabbit in a carrot patch. He had visited the street vendors, and also every social service agency in the neighborhood. Some had not heard about Esperanza; he had corrected that promptly. He brought back several good contacts for us to pursue, plus a couple of job offers for himself. He was so excited to be back in the *barrio*!

This time we talked more seriously. I asked about his spiritual perspectives. Though his background was a little different from most of us, he clearly was one in heart with us. I grilled him on his administrative and public relations experience. We needed his obvious talents and energy. I would need it even more in a month when Mike left. Mike had decided to try a different kind of ministry, and he had given notice that he would leave after his year's commitment. Dr. Joanna Mohn, our new internist, was volunteering a couple of half-days a week, but apart from her I would be the only primary care doctor at Esperanza, as well as both Executive Director and Medical Director.

But where would we get the money to hire David? Together we scratched out a scheme whereby he would counsel half-time, for whatever clients could pay, just as Billy did. The other half-time he would work as my assistant, helping with fundraising, speaking in churches, recruiting volunteers, doing public relations, and supervising some of Coral's and Marialena's work. Perhaps the board would kick in to cover that.

David and his wife Donna flew up for our June board meeting. Their enthusiasm for Esperanza's possibilities captivated the board, just as it had me. The board offered David a job, guaranteeing him a half-time salary for six months. He would have to raise further salary through his own fundraising and counseling efforts.

Before they left town, I brought them home and introduced them to Ron. We had an empty apartment on the third floor of our old Victorian house. Would they like to stay there rent-free for the summer?

On the basis of those offers, David and Donna moved 700 miles to Philadelphia with their two daughters, Angela and Christina.

◆ ◆ ◆ ◆ ◆ ◆ ◆

Right after the anniversary celebration, Ron and I and our children sneaked up to our little cabin in Maine for a couple of badly needed weeks of rest, while Mike graciously extended his commitment to cover for me. Sun and lake breezes and fresh fish and good books in the hammock are tonic for the soul. I came home the end of June thoroughly rested, as ready as I could be for Mike's last day. The Willoughbys had settled into our house while we were gone, and our son David quickly fell in love with his new "big sisters."

A week later I was ready to quit Esperanza. Monday and Tuesday were fifteen-hour days. When the drug program called at about 7 p.m. on Wednesday regarding Victor's strange behavior, I was too tired to deal with it. I told them to bring him to Esperanza in the morning.

By morning his brain damage was extensive and permanent. In my exhaustion I had failed to recognize the warning symptoms of a rapidly progressive toxoplasmosis brain abscess in this young man who I knew had AIDS. Thursday I dumped responsibility for supervising *all* of Marialena's and Coral's work on newly arrived David, as well as some other administrative tasks. Still, Friday and Saturday were difficult, with really sick patients with complicated social and emotional problems.

Two personal matters added to my frustration. Every day, on my subway ride to work, I looked into the basement windows of Wanamaker's department store downtown. They were having a sale on exactly the kind of raincoat I had been wanting but couldn't afford. The sale ended Saturday. My old raincoat was pretty shot—but every single night that week I got off work too late to stop and buy a new one. Also, my kitchen floor was filthy. I was anything but a fanatic on housecleaning, but even I had my limits. I simply did not have one minute all week to scrub that floor, and I knew we couldn't afford a housekeeper.

Sunday morning, after I got home from hospital rounds, our family visited the Diamond Street Mennonite Church across town. Their choir director was giving a farewell concert before moving to Minnesota. Early in the service, the congregation performed a song containing the words, "Lord, I am available to You!" Through clenched teeth I found myself muttering, "Lord, I am NOT available to You! This is too much! If this is what serving You is like, I want out!"

Rather than striking me dead, God bathed me in music. As the racially mixed choir sang song after song, some in gospel tradition, some in other styles, my heart gradually melted. I heard about a God whose love for me cost him more than a raincoat and a dirty floor. I heard about His stooping to enter into our sufferings with us, even as He rules on high.

I wasn't strong enough, or dedicated enough, to save Victor. But God had Victor in His hand. And me. And I could trust Him to rule well in both of our lives. The last song, an unforgettable rendition of "When All God's Children Get Together," described a victory celebration that Victor and I would share someday. Through tears, I began singing with the choir. Victor and I had a hope that superseded AIDS and doctors' errors and messy houses and old coats. It was worth every drop of energy that I had. I left for home ready for the next round.

◆　◆　◆　◆　◆　◆　◆

Monday evening, when I got home from work, the kitchen floor was clean. I couldn't believe it. I had said nothing about that particular frustration. Donna and her two girls had noticed the need as they were putting out the trash, and they decided to bless me by washing the floor. Then Wednesday morning, a beautiful white raincoat appeared on my desk at work. Coral had inherited it from her aunt, couldn't use it, and wondered if it would fit me. It fit perfectly! Whatever God had in mind, clearly He hadn't forgotten me.

As summer progressed, David gradually picked up more of my administrative responsibilities. He also began a weekly Spanish radio talk show, as well as other community outreaches of which I had not even dreamed. He quickly won the respect and trust of board, staff, and community alike. I saw it as a direct reward to his faith that, within a month of his arrival, someone on the board promised to pay 80% of his salary for a year.

Meanwhile, I started feeling less panicked about Dr. Joanna Mohn's pregnancy. Well before her due date, Dr. David Madden, a Christian in the City Health Department, volunteered to cover her eight-week maternity leave. In addition, Dr. David Treviño, an infectious disease specialist from the suburbs, agreed to take weekend call once a month, including hospital rounds. With their help, I was making it.

Then Joanna decided to extend her maternity leave from two to three months. In the third month she decided not to come back at all. Part of me understood and applauded her decision. Had I not been thrilled to stay home after my David was born? The other part of me was not happy at all, especially as it appeared God was NOT providing a substitute. Over the next couple of months, my work-week crept from 60 hours to 65 to 70—up to 74 hours a week. Ron and I were getting to be strangers. When I did have time with my kids, I snapped at them. Something had to give.

In our April meeting, the board decided that David Willoughby would take over my responsibilities as Executive Director, though he still wanted to continue with some of his counseling clients. In spite of the fact that he was young and new to us, clearly he had the makings of a CEO. I would remain as Medical Director and main physician, since I was the only one available to do those jobs. It felt funny giving up public leadership of this organization I had birthed. On the other hand, if God was the real leader, as I had so often proclaimed, He had the right to shift the organizational chart. And He had backed me into a corner. I had to let something go.

Within a week or two of David's appointment as chief, Dr. Mike Moore asked David if he could come back to Esperanza. His experiment in ministry to AIDS patients hadn't turned out as he hoped. Perhaps he could more effectively meet the needs of AIDS patients in the Esperanza setting after all. A week or so later, my stint as solo practitioner was over. I began to wonder if God had set up Mike's months away just to get me out of the top spot.

Why would God want to do that? It couldn't have been my fault that Esperanza was losing money, was it? It certainly wasn't lining my pockets, or those of other staff members. We tried to pay our receptionists and clerical people competitive wages. But the rest of us were living on less than half of what we could have made elsewhere. Patients simply hadn't come in the numbers we had anticipated (though those who did come were sicker than we had dreamed). Medical supplies had cost more than we budgeted. Malpractice rates had skyrocketed. Medicaid wasn't reimbursing well or on time. And it had taken a lot longer than expected to sublet our extra space.

Now that he was really responsible, David pored over our books with Karen. In our first year, we had managed to spend nearly $23,000 more than we had taken in. In our second year, the balance in our bank account had dropped by another $71,000. Despite all of our wonderful patient stories, something was not working well. Over May and June, he had some extended conversations with board members. They began putting out feelers for possible help.

In June, one of them contacted Jack Bennett, of the Foundation for New Era Philanthropy. Jack believed that Christian organizations should be managed even better than secular organizations, that having God on one's side was no excuse for sloppy administration. He was willing to help us get a handle on our situation—if we agreed to let some secular business consultants analyze our operations. He didn't want a group who might be biased towards us because of their own faith. He would pay $10,000 to these consultants for their work, no strings attached.

By mid-July he had hired senior consultants from Shotz, Miller, & Glusman, P.C. to evaluate Esperanza's organizational structure and financial management and to make recommendations for improvement. During the next months, three very professional consultants met personally and in groups with almost everyone at Esperanza. They examined job descriptions, studied billing and collection policies, reviewed accounts receivables, looked at our computer system, and watched what we were actually doing day to day.

Apart from their work, we came to one sad conclusion on our own. In the push to keep Esperanza alive, like many medical organizations before us, we had not given adequate priority to fundraising for health education. Health education was not included in the Robert Wood Johnson grant; all of Coral's salary had been raised separately—when we had time. Now we had no more money to pay her, even though she had done a great job putting on seminars and mentoring trainees from local churches. We simply didn't have the resources both to keep the health center open and continue a community health education program—at least at that time. In September we held a little farewell party and wistfully sent Coral off to another job.

Early in October the consultants met with our staff to go over a long list of areas needing improvement. To remain viable, we would need to make the following major changes, and make them quickly:

1. We needed to improve productivity by 50%. This was not music to the ears of doctors who already were working harder than we ever had in our lives, with patients much sicker and with more complicated illnesses than most suburban doctors would ever see. Mike had already left Esperanza once because he felt the pressure for greater numbers had made him compromise on the quality of the medical and spiritual care he gave. We would have to change job descriptions of nearly everyone, cross-training here, shifting some of the docs' responsibilities off onto other people there, being very disciplined about limiting the time spent with each patient.

2. We had to improve our reporting capacity. Our already out-dated computer system simply couldn't give the information we needed to manage. This was no time to invest in a new computer system, but we could purchase additional software to buy time.

3. We needed radically to increase our daily number of patients. This meant devoting more time to marketing. It also meant scheduling differently. The consultants suggested changes that would work well in a suburban practice, where most people keep appointments. But in our setting, in spite of reminder phone calls, the no-show rate varied from 80% on some days to zero with walk-ins on other days. Double booking would guarantee periodic insanity.

4. We had to improve our collections significantly. In particular, we needed to institute new efficiencies in billing Medicaid, which would not be easy with our antiquated computer system, and we would have to seek new programs with higher reimbursement rates. Perhaps we could join a Medicaid HMO, and pray that no one but our healthier patients would sign up for it.

5. We immediately needed additional board members with organizational, financial, and fundraising skills that we currently lacked. The report stated, *"The administrative leadership appears very dedicated and intelligent, but has less experience than people with which we are familiar in comparable positions."* That stung. We knew we were over our heads, but it was pretty humiliating to have consultants so blatantly call us 'incompetent.' That afternoon after the consultants left, David walked the streets for about four hours, trying to cool down. We both found ourselves saying, "But God, You called us to do this! Did You call us to something You knew we could not do well?"

6. None of the above would help unless we could raise $75,000 in the last six months of our fiscal year, which would end on March 31, 1992. The consultants noted, "…this is greater than the $70,000 raised during the entire previous fiscal year, apart from the Robert Wood Johnson funders." Without this additional money, we would go broke before other changes could benefit us.

To their credit, every staff member committed to do whatever was necessary to accomplish these goals. But some of the goals were beyond us. Our board had only a couple of heavyweights with broad contacts in well-to-do society. Most of them were humble people who were not "well-connected;" they simply wanted to see people helped in their community. How would they respond?

◆   ◆   ◆   ◆   ◆   ◆   ◆

The consultants were scheduled to give their report to the board in mid-October—on my birthday. A few minutes before the meeting, David slipped into my office. Standing with one foot up on a chair, he addressed me solemnly, even tenderly.

"Carolyn, you know that in this meeting the board will have to decide whether to close Esperanza. Are you ready for their decision, either way?"

"David, we *can't* close! Too many people need this place!"

"I know, Carolyn. But for reasons we don't always understand, God sometimes brings Christian ministries to an end. I lived through that, remember?"

I vividly recalled the pain with which David had told me about wrapping up the business matters of the college where he had worked.

"I don't know what God's will is, but I know it is *not* God's will for Esperanza to go bankrupt, leaving our creditors high and dry. If we are going to close, we need to do that *before* we run out of money, so we can pay off everything we owe. That means we may have to make that decision today."

We both stood silently for a moment. Then he continued, gently.

"Carolyn, I know it feels as if Esperanza is your baby. But it's really not. It's God's baby. He can do with it what He wants."

"I know, David. But that's really hard."

"But it's also really important. Remember Abraham's trek up the mountain with his son Isaac?" I had known that Bible story from childhood. God had commanded Abraham to sacrifice his beloved son. God's promises for Abraham's destiny hung on that child and yet God could not bless him fully until he was willing to obey even that command. At the last moment God intervened, telling Abraham to spare his son and providing a ram for the sacrifice instead—but not until Abraham had actually begun to bring the knife down.[34]

I sighed deeply. "You're right. This is God's baby. It never was mine, even from the beginning."

Soberly, we prayed together. Tears smudging my make-up, I asked God's forgiveness for ever thinking that Esperanza was my project. Once again I gave it, and all that it represented, back to God—to do whatever He wanted with it. David prayed more fervently than I had ever heard him pray before. He implored God to do some kind of a miracle and spare Esperanza, but also committed Esperanza to God, whatever He should choose.

Most of the board was already there when David and I took our seats. Fred Estrada, our board president, opened in prayer, then introduced our consultants. Their report was pretty much the same as it had been a week ago to us, with one exception. They subtly pleaded with the board to close Esperanza, implying that it was a good idea that couldn't work. They allowed that the decision could be postponed until year's end. However, it definitely should be closed down then unless Esperanza had made *all* of the suggested organizational improvements and raised $64,000.

I could hardly breathe as I waited for the end of the silence following their presentation. One by one, board members began to comment. Each acknowledged the seriousness of the situation, but didn't see how we could possibly close up shop. Esperanza was too needed by the community and too important for God's kingdom for them to give up. They came to consensus: somehow they would have to rise to the occasion and enable Esperanza to continue.

David and I promised the consultants we would keep them posted. We watched them as they exited through the front door, talking softly and shaking their heads.

---

[34] Gen. 22:1-19

The next day while Karen and I were discussing schedule changes, the phone rang. Leif Beck, founder of a medical management consulting firm and editor of a national newsletter for medical managers, introduced himself. He had volunteered in the past for a Christian health center across town. It had closed, and he missed that type of work. Could he possibly help us?

Could he! We invited him to come down and see Esperanza that afternoon. After the tour, we sat down over coffee and shared the consultants' report. Leif volunteered immediately to bring down to Esperanza, gratis, several colleagues who were specialists in various aspects of medical office management, who would help us make the needed changes. He also agreed to join the board.

A week later David got a call from the Robert Wood Johnson Foundation. Once or twice a year, its entire board of trustees liked to visit projects they had funded, and they would like to visit Esperanza this year. Could that be arranged? Could it ever!

The morning of the meeting there was a major drug bust on our block. Cops were stopping all traffic coming onto 5th Street. Our friends had to park their BMWs and Mercedes' over a block away and walk to Esperanza—past the police frisking several men, past a homeless bag lady, past a spiritualist bookstore, past smiling ex-addicts coming out of the drug program down the hall from us. By the time fifteen of the most influential people in health care had settled themselves in our conference room, they were primed to hear one of our AIDS patients describe what it was like "out there" and how his care at Esperanza was different. We had a wonderful discussion. Towards the end, a number of trustees gave excellent suggestions for raising additional money.

In the following mornings, we gave thanks together for these boons and continued to ask God for His help. We also prayed without detail for especially sick patients and clients receiving counseling. The importance of Esperanza's survival and the gracious power of God began to dominate the consciousness of every staff member. Changes that had seemed impossible began to look feasible. Friction over job turfs disappeared. Little by little, Mike and I were able to let go of time we had been spending talking with patients about non-medical issues, trusting the nurses and counselors to take over that work. Productivity rose.

We made the recommended scheduling changes. David had some unique opportunities to speak in local churches and community groups. Our patient volume began to rise. The days when more patients came than we could possibly see, everyone worked together to make the insanity bearable.

Billing backlog began to drop. We also learned about a program within one of the local HMO's that would reimburse on a cost basis for care of AIDS patients—far more than the $14 per month, regardless of usage, which they gave for other patients. Because we already did more AIDS care than most North Philadelphia providers, it was easy to apply and get approved.

Every week or two David or I would call the consultants to report on events at Esperanza. They were surprised to hear about Leif's joining us the day after the board meeting. They were curious about Esperanza's innovations, though they were a bit patronizing. They were pretty amazed about the Robert Wood Johnson trustees' visit. Then, as money began to come in, I would almost hear puzzled giggles on the other end of the phone as I made my report.

On January 2, David called the consultants to tell them all their recommended changes were complete. In addition, since the board meeting we had received $64,548. He thanked the consultants for their help. Through the phone line he heard, "I don't understand it. This is amazing! I would not have believed it. I... I don't know how you did it! Maybe your God does answer prayer!"

How glad I was that Esperanza was *not* my baby!

Hope on the Streets

"**Y**ou want to do WHAT?"

The young man who had planted himself on the chair in front of my desk repeated matter-of-factly, "Ah'd like to bring forty Christian medical students from Georgia to work with y'all at Esperanza this summer."

By this time my brain had processed his statement enough to realize that forty medical students, forty people of any stripe, could not possibly fit inside the health center at one time. And from Georgia, yet! What did a bunch of southerners from a thousand miles away have to do with Esperanza? Yet the clean-cut, earnest face before me clearly wasn't joking.

"Why don't you tell me a little more about what you have in mind?" I ventured, trying to look as though large groups of Georgians regularly sought to serve our health center.

Bill Pearson had introduced himself to me a week previously, via the phone, as the leader of Medical Campus Outreach. I had never heard of that organization. Now, in December 1991, this tall, dark, early-thirty-something chap began to tell me his story.

He had been a medical student for a year, but then dropped out, believing God was calling him to minister not to patients, but to medical students. He had found practical ways to love and serve dozens of former fellow students, challenging them to pursue relationship with the Great Physician and to model their lives and practices after His. He then trained those who responded to reach out to their friends. By now over a hundred students at the Medical College of Georgia were meeting regularly for mutual spiritual encouragement. But Bill was still not satisfied. These students needed to learn to integrate their faith with their professions in the context of a world in serious need. Somehow he had been referred to Esperanza. He had come to Philadelphia specifically to find us.

After my initial shock, I realized he had a great idea. It would be wonderful to expose students to the likes of Mike Moore, Bill Kussmaul, Phil Siu, and now our new pediatrician, Laura Layer. My colleagues certainly would be refreshing role models for future doctors looking for alternatives to the money-grubbing which colored so much of medical practice. Besides, where in the typical med school curriculum could students learn to integrate medical and spiritual care? If we could help produce a generation of doctors prepared to go where Jesus would go, and heal as Jesus would heal, our little contribution to the Kingdom would be multiplied many times over.

Still, we could not pack forty more bodies inside Esperanza.

While Bill talked, my eyes drifted to a stack of junk mail on my desk. The top piece was a memo from the city's Infant Immunization Initiative, better known as the I-3 plan. My mind wandered to the measles epidemic that had been ravaging Philadelphia since the beginning of the year. Nine children had died, and 1500 more had become sick from an entirely preventable disease. Now panicked, the city Health Department was trying to muster "all hands on deck" to combat Philadelphia's horrendous immunization statistics. Some 70% of the two-year-olds in our area were behind on their shots. Our social worker, Marialena Gant, had been our representative at I-3 meetings, and had coordinated our special "free shots for tots" days.

Suddenly, the two images—medical students and measles—came together, as if I had just awakened from a daze and refocused my eyes. I grabbed my phone and buzzed Marialena. "Could you possibly come down to my office for a few minutes?"

After quick introductions, Marialena plopped herself onto the sofa. "What's up, boss?"

"Bill, here, needs a place for forty medical students to work, where they can learn to meet both physical and spiritual needs. The city has a need to get vaccinations to kids who aren't plugged into the health system. What do you think about using his students to take immunizations door to door?"

"That's a great idea!" Marialena bubbled.

"That sounds good to me!" Bill exclaimed.

"Well now, let's think about what would have to happen to make this possible. First, we'd have to be able to get vaccines from the City."

"That's no problem. They'd be thrilled," Marialena assured us.

"Of course, we'd have to make sure all the students are fully trained about the indications for the vaccines and their side effects. And the legal issues involved. And the paper work. And the OHSA[35] regulations about handling needles. Of course any one giving vaccines or holding kids would

---

[35] Office of Safety and Health Administration of the U.S. Government

themselves have to be immunized against Hepatitis B. And we'd need licensed doctors supervising them. Hmmm. I don't think we could spare Esperanza docs to do that."

"I think we could get a half-dozen docs from Georgia to take vacation time to come and work with us," Bill offered.

"OK, though we'd have to get Pennsylvania medical licenses for them." I mused.

"And refrigeration on the streets for the vaccines." Marialena added.

"And translators for the students who don't speak Spanish," I tacked on.

"Translation? That's the least of our worries. These are suburban kids, are they not?" Marialena glanced at Bill. "How are they going to survive on our streets?"

I thought of the possible consequences if one of the students should innocently try to photograph a drug deal, or otherwise violate the rules of the *barrio*.

Quickly our list of requirements grew. We'd need to orient them to the Latino culture and instruct them on safety. We'd need street-wise translators, sensitive to the spiritual issues the students would unearth. We'd also need space for the students to live and meet together, a way to feed and transport them, a van from which immunizations could be given block to block, emergency supplies, and translated materials. We'd need cooperation from the police department and of other community agencies. We'd especially need the partnership of local churches with whom we had already worked, so the folk we identified with spiritual needs could receive follow-up after the students left. Bill himself had a long list of jobs to do in Georgia, not the least of which was to arrange to get these students and physicians to Philadelphia by July 1. We'd also need finances for the whole operation.

Eventually, we had listed all the items we could think of. No one spoke. Finally, I turned to Marialena.

"Well, Red, are you up for this?"

"Who, me?" she squealed.

"I can't think of a better person to put this all together!"

"This is an incredible list. For all of this to get done between now and next summer would take some pretty big miracles."

"Well, do you think this is God's idea, or not?"

We all sat for a moment and looked at each other. Slowly Marialena said, "I think God *is* in this." She paused for a long minute. "And if He is, then I guess I'd better be, too."

◆ ◆ ◆ ◆ ◆ ◆ ◆

By February, Esperanza's board had committed itself to the project, which we decided to call the Summer Medical Institute, or SMI. The Philadelphia Health Department was skeptical but desperate enough to give us the vaccines. The eight churches with whom we had worked most closely were more enthusiastic. Each pastor mapped out the blocks around his church for which his congregation would take responsibility to care for persons expressing spiritual needs. Even more encouraging, they began recommending key teenagers in their youth groups who would be apt translators. Marialena chose thirteen of these young people, and put together a program to train them in basic interpersonal and leadership skills and in Christian discipleship. Realizing that many of these kids would have to give up chances for summer employment, she promised $15 a day—nowhere near what a real job would have paid, but better than nothing.

Finding a place for the students to stay was a bit tougher. All of Marialena's leads in North Philadelphia proved to be blind alleys. In late May, Bill in Augusta managed to arrange for the students to stay in fraternity houses at the University of Pennsylvania. Transportation to North Philly would involve a forty-five minute ride on the subway, elevated train, and bus, but that in itself would be educational.

Marialena and I marveled as hundreds of logistical details fell into place. We still weren't sure about the financial aspects. We had a few small grants from pharmaceutical companies and a couple of foundations. Bill's share was trickling in from grandmothers and Sunday school classes in the Southeast. Nonetheless, we had quite a ways to go.

Just before the students were to arrive, we received an unexpected boon. Billy Graham was scheduled to begin a week-long crusade in Veterans' Stadium on June 22. The day before the crusade, he wanted to visit one Christian ministry in Philadelphia and another in Camden, just across the river in New Jersey. Would it be all right if he visited Esperanza?

Would it!

Early that morning the police erected barricades along the curb in front of Esperanza to reserve parking spaces for Billy Graham's entourage. Slowly the motorcade wound its way up 5th Street, amidst the odors of *tostones* and *pastelillos* wafting from street vendors. Because his Parkinson's disease was making it difficult for him to climb stairs, we had arranged to borrow a room on the first floor right below us. We had put enough chairs in a circle for Dr. Graham, those accompanying him, several of our staff, the directors of a couple of other agencies, and one of our patients. I didn't dream how many reporters and photographers would crowd around our circle.

David Willoughby, our executive director, introduced everyone. Briefly I shared our vision for touching bodies, souls, and spirits with God's love and power, and the special ways we were doing this in the areas of children's needs, mental illness, drug abuse, and AIDS. Speaking in Spanish while David translated, our patient vividly described the demeaning treatment he had received elsewhere when people had learned of his AIDS and mental illness. "Esperanza is so different. The doctors have really helped me. But it's not just that. Here they treat me like family," he concluded. Then we asked Dr. Graham for his questions and comments.

Whatever disease processes were at work in his body, they had not diminished the intellectual acuity of this warrior of the faith. His piercing blue eyes looked from one to another, connecting deeply with each of us. Finally he spoke.

"I am not worthy to untie the sandals of the men and women who work here. What you are doing is the real work of the Kingdom. It is far more significant in God's eyes than anything I do."

I gasped. This was the last thing I expected him to say. If any Christian leader was worthy of honor, it was Billy Graham. But he was as humble as he was illustrious, as genuine up close as he seemed before millions.

With a few more words he encouraged us, offered to connect us with some resources through his son Franklin, then closed the meeting by praying for us. As his escorts hustled him off to his appointment in New Jersey and cameras clicked all around, he shook hands with everyone. Our photographer happened to catch the moment when he gave me a big hug. That photo, still on my desk, remains one of my most treasured possessions.

We found out a bit later that the Love in Action committee for his Philadelphia Crusade decided to pick up Esperanza's part of the Summer Medical Institute's costs.

◆ ◆ ◆ ◆ ◆ ◆ ◆

That week held one more poignant event. David had submitted his resignation as executive director, mostly because his administrative responsibilities had deflected him too far from the counseling role to which he felt called. He and his family were moving to Arizona at the end of the week. On his last day at Esperanza, tears flowed freely. He had become a trusted leader and dear friend to nearly everyone.

Karen and I especially would feel his absence. Until a new executive director could be found, the weight of leadership would once again settle on our shoulders. The words of Job flashed through my mind, "The Lord giveth and the Lord taketh away. Blessed be the name of the Lord."[36] *Easy to say; not so easy to mean. God, help me to trust you once more.*

The next week, just after Dr. Graham's successful crusade, forty medical and nursing students arrived from Georgia. We held orientation at the University of Pennsylvania for two days before we took them into the neighborhood where they would serve. We discussed immunization protocols, the overall health status of Philadelphia, and Puerto Rican history and culture. The discussion on safety precautions took some unexpected turns. A police officer demonstrated how to stand to the side of a door after knocking on it, to avoid being shot if the knock were answered by gunfire. Talk about inspiring confidence!

The next day, North Philly pastors calmed fears as they addressed evangelism in the context of the *barrio*. Nonetheless, by the end of the neighborhood tour from the safety of the vans ("That guy is selling drugs. That guy over there is a pimp. Those two girls are prostitutes, who probably live and work in that abandoned house across the street....") the students were suffering culture shock. It was only partly relieved by the delicious Puerto Rican dinner provided by a local church. The students' prayers before they began work the next morning took on particular fervency.

That morning I made it a point to be with them on the streets. It interested me that Marialena and her pastors chose to begin on the corner of the now-closed Medicaid mill where my adventures in North Philadelphia had started. On both sides of the treeless streets, I could see rows of brick houses interrupted only by an occasional empty and dilapidated

---

[36] Job 1:21 KJV

factory, burned-out dwelling, or garbage-strewn lot. I was glad to meet the pediatrician from Georgia who was using his vacation time to staff the van, now parked in the middle of the block between vandalized cars. I chatted briefly with the students working with him and the couple manning the paperwork table. As Marialena assigned a translator to each pair of white-coated medical students and sent them off to knock on doors, I talked to TV cameramen and reporters from the *Philadelphia Inquirer*. Then I stood back to watch.

The first six doors opened slightly then rapidly slammed in the students' faces. Finally, at the seventh house, the mother actually listened and got her immunization records. She and her six children tramped down to the waiting van. Within minutes, the doors of the first six houses opened again. Mothers and children poured out.

While a couple of students prepared the shots, three of the guys began playing with the kids. Soon they became living jungle gyms, with giggling children hanging from every arm and leg. Other doors opened. Even after receiving shots and lollipops, the kids hung around. Conversations developed in all directions: children and students sat on the cracked sidewalk; moms and female students sat on porches; old men and male students chatted on the corners. Even peanut-butter and jelly sandwiches, eaten in the slim shade of a building or on curbs covered with broken glass and used crack caps, tasted good to the students. Children followed afternoon teams on their rounds, holding onto their hands and chatting in Spanish. By the end of the day, the students were falling in love with North Philadelphia, despite the police warnings.

In mid-afternoon a couple of well-dressed young men with heavy gold jewelry approached to find out how long we intended to stay. They were cordial, and expressed appreciation that we had vaccinated their children. However, our presence past four o'clock would interfere with business on the corner. We smiled and agreed to clean up before then.

◆　◆　◆　◆　◆　◆　◆

The second week the group ventured onto Hope Street, ironically one of the city's worst drug areas. Every morning the students prayed for protection—for those giving immunizations and those going door to door—

and for a safe parking spot. One morning, a drug dealer watched the driver jockey into a spot in the middle of the block, and then sauntered over.

"Hey, man, are you the docs giving kids shots?" he asked in accented English.

The senior coordinator nodded, trying not to stare at the tattoos on the man's arms. The man thrust his bejeweled hands into the pocket of his jeans.

"I'm Crazy Ace, and this is my corner." The coordinator was about to explain that the team would stay down the block, but she didn't get the chance. "I like what you're doing," he continued. "Pull your van in here. I'll make sure nobody bothers you!"[37]

And no one did. Nor did anyone throughout the summer. The white coats, which seemed so bizarre in the context of graffiti-lined streets, seemed to assure residents that our students were not narcotics agents, not missionaries from cults, not a problem at all.

The days flew by. Some days the students gave out more than 100 shots. They worked out a system so that kids needing three or four shots could get them all at the same instant, to minimize crying. They took pains to get the names of the children's regular doctors and to encourage mothers to follow up with them. Other days would be quieter, leaving the van staff open to take in colorful scenes of life in a Puerto Rican neighborhood, interwoven with sights and sounds of the drug culture. Students were often invited into homes for coffee or Coke, where they listened to stories of the *barrio*, laughed and wept with their new friends, and sometimes explained their hope in Christ.

Many conversations had eternal significance. Student evaluations recorded the following vignettes:

I was talking with two children sitting on a curb and telling them about Jesus. When I told them that God loves them, one little boy's eyes opened real wide. His only response was an amazed "God loves me?"

A woman with four children, all with some medical problem, was very open to hearing the Gospel. We left her, promising to return the

---

[37] This incident was originally reported by Dr. Ned Rupp in "Taking Hope to Hope Street," *Physicians Magazine*, March/April 1993, pp. 14-16.

following Monday to give her son shots. When I returned, she told me how she had accepted Christ that night in the quiet of her own bedroom.

As I walked up to the van, Wendy told me that Joel and Todd needed someone to drive a drug addict to a rehabilitation center. I was happy to do this, but immediately doubted, knowing how few drug addicts are actually ready to seek help. To my surprise, within a minute Todd, Joel, and Sam (not his real name), suitcase in hand, emerged from the building. As I put Sam's suitcase in the car, one of the dealers across the street began to take interest in the situation. "Sam, where you goin'? You owe us money, you know." Propelled by the cackles of his buddies, the dealer crossed over to our side. With dread I saw him taking off his watch. "No, Lord," I prayed as I saw Sam taking off his glasses. The dealer was backing him up against a wall pushing him by his shoulders. "Where do you think you are going?" He swung, hitting Sam squarely in the mouth. I looked down not wanting to see the next swing. Joel had clenched his fists. Todd stood perfectly still. The dealer hit Sam a second time in the face, the sound of flesh and bone coming together silencing even the dealer's friends across the street. Hatred welled up in me, as I looked at the 275 pound body of the well-tanned young dealer and the frail, 130-pound body of this little man who looked 60. Fear also came. Were we safe? Sam fell down to his knees as blood flowed from his mouth. He was hit again. I heard the blood hit the sidewalk, a sound I had heard before only in the context of an emergency room. "Stop!" I prayed silently. Suddenly the dealer turned and went back across the street as deliberately as he had come. We helped Sam off the sidewalk, blood still flowing, and into the back seat of our car. Todd and Joel sat on either side of him, and Todd had his arm around him. We did not speak except for directions. We had suddenly been given a glimpse into the deep spiritual battle that was being waged. As we entered the rehab center, two Hispanics in their early twenties greeted us. Sam, an African American, sat down. They warned him, "If you come here you will change, but only because God will be changing you. Is that what you want?" For the first time, through swollen lips and rotted teeth, I saw Sam smile. "Yes, I want that. It is time for that." I realized that

I would have passed Sam by on the street as hopeless, but that God had planned to bring Sam to Himself....

♦   ♦   ♦   ♦   ♦   ♦   ♦

The days were emotionally intense. In addition to the hard work on the sweltering streets and the cultural challenges, the students found themselves facing new questions. Who was to blame for all these problems? Who could say he was completely innocent? If communication through translators was so frustrating to them, how must the Spanish-speakers feel day after day as they struggle to survive in an English-speaking world? When they returned to the South, would a caring Christian remain to minister to their new friends? Some days their emotions flipped in rapid succession from compassion to anger, to deep awareness of the surrounding hopelessness, to fear as violence brushed too closely, to joy at God's presence in odd places.

Besides being on the streets, each day two students took their turn following doctors around at Esperanza. They watched us break HIV-positive diagnoses to patients, confront manipulators, instruct illiterate elderly, and comfort the despondent, as well as deal with the usual complexity of poverty-related health problems. They saw first-hand the tight interrelation of physical and spiritual health, and how caring for one would lead naturally to caring for the other. During breaks we tried to answer the questions they had accumulated about integrating their faith into their practices. They also enjoyed our air conditioning—a big contrast from the 95° heat and 95% humidity they were experiencing on the asphalt outside.

In the evenings, students sometimes joined the Spanish congregations to which they were assigned or spent time with local medical students. Philadelphia students seemed encouraged and challenged by our visitors. Other evenings the SMI students met at the frat houses in small discipleship groups or in workshops led by visiting faculty. In between, they worked on developing their own personal life vision. Ron had some deep discussions with students on practical implications for the theology of the Kingdom of God. One week he and I did a seminar on Christian marriage. In addition, I think there were some other things going on. Just after SMI concluded, several students announced their engagements!

♦   ♦   ♦   ♦   ♦   ♦   ♦

The last week, while the final shots were being given, we invited city health officials, participating pastors, and representatives from sponsoring pharmaceutical companies to a meeting on August 14 in one of the University's lecture halls. One student put together a wonderful slide show, with pictures of the work, statistics, and testimonials from other students. When the student leaders began talking about the numbers, I watched the eyes of the health officers grow as big as guavas. In 27 days of actual house-to-house visitation the SMI team had knocked on over 2400 doors, evaluated the vaccination status of 2373 children, and given 1743 vaccines to 737 children.

After the presentation, the city health commissioner, Dr. Bob Ross, took the microphone. "I must confess I was pretty skeptical when I heard what you guys were planning. But I am astonished—at what you have accomplished, and at the maturity, professionalism, and cross-cultural sensitivity that you have demonstrated. Without question, you reached a good number of children who had fallen through the cracks of the health care system. And you have done so in a way that will facilitate follow-up. The good will you have generated will remain for a long time.

"More than this, through this summer program, you've learned things way beyond what most physicians gain in their entire medical education and thirty years of practice. I commend you for making this investment.

"When I really look at what you have done in these six weeks, I realize that you have accomplished things the City Health Department could never do. You're giving out more than shots. And North Philly needs more than shots. I know of a drug program sponsored by some religious people in North Philly that has done more good than any of the city drug programs. Why? Let's just call it the..." He hesitated, turning slightly red, then continued. "The 'J' factor. Now I'm not particularly religious, or anything, but it's clear that programs with that kind of spiritual emphasis help people on a deeper level than what we have to offer. We in government cannot even talk about that kind of thing. But you ought to document what you are doing, then lobby the government to support this! It's really remarkable!"

Later that year I saw an example of how remarkable the Summer Medical Institute and its "J factor" were. In October, a 35-year-old woman whom I shall call Lydia came to Esperanza for a pre-employment physical exam. While taking her history, I learned that medical students Jamie Flanders and Steven Presley had visited her that summer to ask about the immunization status of her children. All three of her kids were up-to-date on their shots. The students had asked how they could pray for her. They stayed for an hour while she poured out her heart, as she had never done with anyone before. A few days later they returned for another long visit. She never saw them again, yet those two visits had brought new hope into her life. Though she had never held a job before, she had sought employment and was ready to start working the following Monday. Apparently God's agenda for SMI was bigger than shots, bigger than "saving souls." He was truly bringing healing in all areas of people's lives.

◆　◆　◆　◆　◆　◆　◆

The following year, the Philadelphia Health Department developed an immunization program incorporating some of the approaches used by the SMI. It sent an army of high school and college students and faculty members of local universities into neighborhoods, rather than asking tired moms to come to immunization offices. We were glad to see the increased effectiveness of the City program. During that summer the City was able to give shots to 3,000 children, at a cost of about $1,100,000. That year, however, SMI gave nearly 2000 shots to 828 children, at a cost of $60,000. It hit me that Kingdom medicine is cost-effective medicine, effective on a large scale as well as in the office.

The summer of 1993 the students added asthma and anemia screenings to their offer of immunizations. We were shocked to discover that nearly a third of the children in our neighborhoods in North Philadelphia had signs of asthma, a finding confirmed by other researchers that year. The next year they also began to screen for lead poisoning, a brain-destroying tragedy all too common in areas where houses have old paint and plumbing. In subsequent years they added screening for high blood pressure and diabetes and gave out hundreds of bicycle helmets to children. They also tested hundreds of people for HIV infection and followed them up. After giving 16,907 shots, the last couple of years they decided not even to do immunizations. By then most children were up to date and their own doctors were doing a better job of keeping them that way. Beginning in 2002, the team decided not to work in Philadelphia at all, but in a Texas-Mexico border area, where the need for their services was greater.

During the ten years that Summer Medical Institutes remained in Philadelphia, they proved to be one of the most effective means for connecting spiritually needy people to local churches that North Philly had ever seen.

The first summer, despite the students' low-pressure approach, their conversations led people in over 442 homes to request a follow-up visit from someone in a local church. Eleven recorded "decisions for Christ." By the second or third summer, SMI students were uncovering spiritual need, praying with folk, and watching people move significantly closer to God more than 100 times a week. We thanked God for our partnership with local churches. We prayed hard that God would help them rise to this huge task of follow-up.

Neighborhood people were not the only ones who benefited spiritually from SMI. I read dozens of comments from student evaluations like these:

It has greatly decreased my desire for personal gain in my career (money, possessions, etc.) and increased my desire to give of myself to God.

It has made me think about whether working in a middle class world is the best use of my skills.

It has shown me a need I didn't know was so huge.

It has taught me that prayer is war.

It showed me the importance of treating the "whole" person and that sharing your faith isn't as complicated as I tended to make it.

It showed me how much God loves everyone, not just the "nice, clean" people.

It showed me I can be a better doctor because of my Christianity, and vice versa. There is scant separation between physical and spiritual health.

I've learned it is possible to share your faith in a health care setting. And that God's work will never lack God's supply.

It has helped teach me not to limit what God possibly has planned for me—not to settle for mediocrity—to dream big!

It was life-changing and habit forming.

I guess it has been habit forming. As of this writing, 421 students from 65 different medical schools have participated in the Philadelphia Summer Medical Institutes and their successors, the Texas/Mexico Institutes. Many have earned academic credit. Of these, 120 returned for a second or third summer with SMI, and 85 have done medical rotations in more than 45 nations.

SMI has been reproduced, mostly by alumni, in several other cities in the United States, as well as in Ecuador, Mexico, Peru, Venezuela, Zambia, Philippines, Dominican Republic, Honduras, Indonesia, Kenya and Bangladesh. One alumnus has settled permanently in Kazakstan, where he does family practice and teaches Kazak medical students to practice medicine Jesus-style. At least four others have settled into practices among underserved populations in the United States. Over forty are actively involved across the country in challenging the next generations of medical students to develop the character and competencies needed to lead in health professions and to change the world for Jesus Christ. Their goal is to raise up a new generation of health care providers who are Christ-centered and biblically integrated in their approach to the healing arts. With a cumulative total of more than 2,000 students who have participated in these different projects around the globe, their vision is beginning to be fulfilled

I never dreamed we'd be looking at these results the day Bill Pearson walked into my office. But neither did I begin to imagine the richness and joy God planned to bring us through the empty office in the front of our building, which we needed to sublet.

An Unexpected Harvest

"And here are additional potential counseling rooms, should you need to expand later," I explained to the tall man with graying hair who followed me down the hall.

"This is great! I'll take it!" Bill Campbell exclaimed. "Say, once we get New Journeys in Recovery set up, would you be interested in doing physical exams for our clients?"

"I think that could be arranged!" I was only too glad that finally, after months of standing empty, our extra rooms would get a rent-paying tenant. And it would be convenient to have an outpatient drug program right on our premises. It certainly would complement our efforts to provide care for the whole person.

Bill was determined to get a state license for his fledgling drug program. Though he was a Christian, New Journeys would be a secular program, meaning it would hire staff without regard for religious background. Nonetheless, most of his counselors turned out to be Christians, perhaps because no one else would work in that neighborhood for such low pay.

Early in 1990, Esperanza and New Journeys in Recovery were not the only new programs in North Philadelphia. A number of local pastors, profoundly burdened about problems associated with the drug culture, were beginning their own residential drug treatment programs. Some were in church annexes, some in renovated storefronts and factories, and some in homes. All were staffed by religious workers and reformed drug addicts. These leaders had heard of the phenomenal success of Teen Challenge, a religiously-based program begun in the 1950s. A government study had shown that 86% of former drug abusers were drug free seven years after completing Teen Challenge's one year program.[38] These results far surpassed

---

[38] United States Department of Health, Education, and Welfare, Public Health Service, Alcohol, Drug Abuse, and Mental Health Administration, National Institute on Drug Abuse, "An Evaluation of the Teen Challenge Treatment Program," Services Research Report (Washington, D.C.: Government Printing Office, 1977)

those of most secular programs. The pastors wanted to duplicate that success closer to home and in a more Latino context.

I admired these leaders' sacrificial dedication. Some invested their life savings in the programs. Many were on call practically 24 hours a day. They cared deeply about the devastation that drugs had brought to their neighborhoods and to the men and women who came for help. And they frequently saw major changes in those who opened themselves to God's help.

However, they often had little or no training in counseling or in dealing with the complicated issues connected to drug abuse. On their own, they could not meet state standards for a drug treatment program. They were glad to hear of a licensed facility where their residents could obtain services required by the state, from counselors who were at least sympathetic to their religious views. Before long, the New Journeys' waiting room was packed with residents from Shepherd House, Way to Heaven Ministries, Soldiers of the Lord, Refuge in Christ, Fountain of Hope, and other local programs.

Since these men and women needed physical exams before they could begin official treatment, many found their way into Esperanza. Some brought well-honed skills of manipulation, coercion, deception, and verbal abuse. Our receptionists and nurses often felt badgered and conned.

"But your director promised Mr. Campbell I could be seen today!"

"Our director is not in right now, so I can't check with him. But honestly, we have a full schedule this afternoon."

"But this is an emergency. I am really sick! I've had high fever and chills for two days!"

"But your temperature is normal now!"

"That's because I just took some Tylenol. If you don't let me see the doctor, you're going to be really sorry!.... And I'm going to report your stupid clinic for Medicaid fraud!...."

A telephone disappeared from an exam room early on, and a vacuum cleaner from our closet a few weeks later. We had a number of team meetings, and meetings with Mr. Campbell, to establish procedures minimizing the addicts' disruptiveness.

However, we also witnessed another side of addiction. By the time we saw them, a lot of our addicts had been drug free for a while, and had been in local programs long enough to understand the basics of the Gospel. Many were far more open to thinking about spiritual issues than they had ever been in their entire lives, whether they thought in Christian, Jewish, or Muslim terms. Some had had dramatic conversions. Many felt a deep gratitude that God was delivering them from a problem that was destroying them. Their braggadocio was gone. In its place was a simple delight in awakening sober every morning and feeling "normal."

"You know, doc, I can't tell you how good it feels to be 'clean' again. I was on those streets for a long, long time, and it was hell," Jaime told me. "Now I'm eating three times a day, and starting to feel decent, and thinking straight. I'm getting back a little self-respect. And I'm learning stuff I never knew, about God and stuff. I'm starting to think about the future, and maybe making something of my life." On the way out of the exam room he paused. "Thanks, doc. I really appreciate all you guys have done for me."

Mixed with their joy was a lot of anguish. Reynaldo had not been there for his mom while she lingered with cancer. Now she was gone, and he could not tell her how sorry he was for all he had put her through. Carla's four kids had been in foster care for years. One had been sexually abused and had gone from foster home to foster home. None of them wanted to come home with her now. George's wife wanted nothing more to do with him. Allen had held a high-paying job in the stock market until he got hooked on cocaine. They all assessed their losses and grieved over what they had done to themselves and their families.

Others wrestled with fear of the future, as insecurities and incompetencies were unmasked. Though he had prospered as a drug lord, Ricardo had never really learned to read. How could he earn a living honestly? Sarah wondered who would ever marry her, now that she was infertile from repeated episodes of gonorrhea.

Some had used drugs to cover the pain of bereavement, abandonment, abuse, or neglect. Now, without drugs, they had to deal with the tormenting memories they had tried to escape. Jose's program director sent him to see me because he was unable to sleep more than an hour or two a night, even though he was exhausted. As we talked, I realized he was severely depressed. The son of two alcoholics, he had lived with abuse and hopelessness ever since he could remember. He had used drugs as self-medication for his lifelong depression—and now the drugs were gone. Another director brought in Willie because he didn't want to sleep. Willie confided that sleep inevitably brought nightmares, flashbacks to the night that drug lords gunned their way into his row house and murdered his father while he watched.

As these types of stories surfaced, sometimes I just listened, and wept a bit with the patient. Sometimes I offered an anti-depressant or other medication. Sometimes I pointed out that God was angry at their abusers, too. In fact, He considered the attitudes prompting the abuse as worthy of a death sentence. If the perpetrators refused to accept the justice of that verdict and the gracious sacrifice Jesus made on their behalf, they certainly would be held accountable and have to pay up. Over and over I watched such simple truths brighten glazed-over eyes.

◆ ◆ ◆ ◆ ◆ ◆ ◆

I liked caring for Mr. Campbell's clients. I got a thrill out of seeing how drastically God was changing some of them.

Sometimes they ministered to *me*. On a day that I came to work tired and discouraged, Jorge was on the schedule for a drug program physical. While I was taking his history, he started telling me what he had discovered in his Bible study the day before. He enthusiastically recounted the story of Jesus calming the storm and shared how Jesus was calming the storms in his own life. Jorge had been a believer all of four weeks, but his transparent joy spoke volumes about my need to trust God with my own problems. I left the exam room strangely refreshed.

I realized we could help these men and women in crucial ways. Under the best of circumstances, rehabilitation from drug abuse is difficult. In the tightly structured, overcrowded situations where these men and women lived, it could be particularly frustrating. Sometimes program staff made decisions that seemed arbitrary. Sometimes they weren't terribly sophisticated in understanding their clients' special needs. The Esperanza docs often acted as sounding boards, where recovering addicts could express frustrations without being punished. Sometimes just listening, giving a few words of encouragement, and maybe praying with them would prevent their leaving the program. Other times we got on the phone and spoke to their program staff, gently advocating for our patients. We had after-hours conversations with their directors, explaining why using medicines does not indicate a lack of faith in God, and why coming to Christ doesn't necessarily cure chronic mental illness.

Many long-term addicts did finish these local programs and go to the Teen Challenge farm in Rehresburg, PA, for the "second stage" of rehabilitation, which included vocational training. We saw many when they graduated and returned to Philly. Unfortunately, those who didn't get into local churches for nurture and accountability often relapsed. Religious experience alone, apart from the support of a healthy community, didn't seem to cure addiction for very long. We found ourselves encouraging church attendance as well as checking liver function tests. Those who did get into good churches did much better. Some even became leaders in the community.

On the other hand, just because these addicts were receiving new life spiritually and emotionally didn't mean that they were exempt from the physical effects of past choices. One in three of Mr. Campbell's clients had evidence of chronic hepatitis C infection, which, if untreated, could lead to liver failure or liver cancer. Maria, at age 24, would have a weak heart the rest of her life because of a massive heart attack suffered while on cocaine. Oliver would need skin grafting for deep ulcers where his injection sites had gotten infected. Leon had severe alcoholic nerve damage to his feet. Oscar suffered renal failure because he had not taken care of his diabetes and hypertension during his addiction. Most of the women had female concerns, often related to the prostitution by which they had sustained their addiction.

And some patients already had HIV infection. Some months we had to break that news to as many as six people.

Drug addicts were not the only ones at risk. I had the heart-wrenching task of telling a beautiful teenage girl that she was HIV positive two days before her senior prom, and of giving the same news to an 81-year-old gentleman who had been "fooling around a bit" since his wife died a couple of years before. The virus didn't discriminate. We learned that, even apart from drug use, *any* sexual activity with someone who had ever had sex with someone else after 1978 put a person at risk, even if condoms were used. We learned to ask probing questions about risk factors to *every* patient. We were startled to find how many ordinary people were at risk.

Thus, fairly suddenly, we became one of the area's major providers of HIV care. Dr. Mike Moore, not too far out of his residency, was good at AIDS care from the beginning. I had to scramble to catch up by attending HIV conferences. Dr. David Treviño, the infectious disease specialist who volunteered regularly, helped us a lot. Later, so would Dr. Bryan Hollinger and Dr. Ramon Gadea. All along, the specialists at Episcopal Hospital shared their knowledge with us as they helped us care for our in-patients. Our sheer volume of HIV-positive patients was guaranteed to make us experts, well before government funding would make HIV care an attractive specialty for health centers. I was not surprised to hear, years later, that Esperanza was the first Philadelphia community health center to be designated a Center of Excellence for HIV Care by Health Partners of Philadelphia.

◆　◆　◆　◆　◆　◆　◆

One of the first things we learned about AIDS is that it affects every aspect of a person's life. Long before physical symptoms develop, it affects relationships. Carmen's family threw her out when they heard her diagnosis. Alicia's co-workers avoided her at coffee break. Jerry's church suddenly turned cold towards him, saying he was under the judgment of God.

Every time I heard that sort of thing, I got angry. AIDS certainly was not always a consequence of bad behavior. Even when it was, there was a big difference between "consequence" and "judgment." Was lung cancer "judgment" on a smoker? Was a heart attack "judgment" on the steak lover? Even if AIDS were in some way God's judgment, Jesus had little patience with those who held themselves superior to people under judgment. In fact, the warning he gave the bystanders was downright scary. *"Do you suppose that these Galileans were greater sinners than all other Galileans because they suffered this fate? I tell you, no, but unless you repent, you will all likewise perish."*[39]

Even if a person with AIDS were suffering from his own choices, which of us would not eventually do the same? Those who prated self-righteously about "people with AIDS" seemed to forget that we all will die. We will all suffer the consequences of Adam's and Eve's sin and of our own—whether through AIDS or some other means. From God's viewpoint, how could I be so sure that Jerry's drug use was worse than my hatred, or that Carmen's promiscuity was worse than my gossip? Jesus once pointed out that a cheating tax collector who admitted his own need for mercy would be forgiven long before a self-righteous religious leader.[40]

When I read the Bible, I saw Jesus loving people, regardless of their sin. He didn't condone their sin; in fact, he spent plenty of energy confronting

---

[39] Luke 13:2,3
[40] Luke 17:9-14

people about their lifestyles. However, He still reached out with compassion and grace.

Sometimes the social ostracism experienced by my patients had nothing to do either with morality or with facts. I remembered Juan telling me his family would serve him on paper plates while everyone else ate on china. I didn't fully believe Carlos' stories until I interviewed him on a Spanish radio station. After we finished, I watched the station operator carefully use alcohol to wipe off the microphone Carlos had used. No wonder our AIDS patients appreciated our hugs so much.

These social difficulties were based, tragically enough, on ignorance. Effects of HIV within a marital relationship were not. I personally cared for seven or eight couples in which one person was HIV-positive and the other was not, whose condoms had broken. One young wife got pregnant even though her HIV-positive husband was using double condoms! We learned of researchers who had documented that HIV transmission occasionally occurs despite consistent condom use. Their work had not been published because of death threats. I could understand why David's fiancée promptly broke their engagement when she found out about his HIV infection. But that made it no less painful for David.

If struggling with a fatal disease were not enough to affect a person emotionally, these kinds of events certainly would be. We walked with patients through denial, rage, anxiety, depression, and paranoia.

HIV infection also sometimes limited career options. Could Mariana sign up for nursing school, knowing she was HIV-positive? Would Frank lose his construction job on some flimsy excuse when his boss found out his HIV status? We knew of such incidents, even though that kind of discrimination was illegal. What of James' fears that he would not be strong enough to work and support his family? Most of our patients did not have disability insurance policies. What they gained from Social Security disability would not be enough to pay for their medicines, let alone support a whole family.

The diagnosis of HIV/AIDS had other financial implications. A currently uninsured person probably would never qualify for life or disability insurance – perhaps not even health insurance. If a person stopped working, gave away all his assets, and went on welfare, he might qualify for Medicaid. But welfare checks alone would not be desirable income for many people.

Educationally handicapped people, of whom our neighborhood had plenty, presented a special challenge. They frequently could not read the literature provided by our colleagues in the AIDS prevention agencies. Even with repeated explanations, many could not comprehend that ordinary sex between two people who look and feel well could be lethal. Once they were infected, they had difficulty understanding how to use simple medications, let alone the new anti-HIV drugs with their complicated and critical dosing instructions. My heart went out to people who could not speak English. Thank God our providers spoke Spanish. But what of the people who spoke one of the other fifty-eight languages used in Philadelphia?

As they neared life's end, people with HIV infection dealt with even more issues. Parents had to arrange for guardians for their kids. People without supportive families wondered where they could live when they got too sick to be independent. Many patients faced a total absence of good options.

Through the kindness of the drug program where he lived, Vincent was allowed to stay there for many months after his rehab was completed. The day came, however, when he began to require more care than the staff could provide. We looked in vain for some place in Philadelphia where he could live, let alone a place where someone could understand his Spanish. Every nursing home accepting AIDS patients had a months-long waiting list. Finally he decided to return to his native Puerto Rico. He died less than 24 hours after his plane landed.

◆   ◆   ◆   ◆   ◆   ◆   ◆

In addition to all of their other difficulties, people with HIV infection often don't feel well. They struggle with mouth ulcers, annoying skin rashes, painful muscle disorders, chronic diarrhea, frequent sinus infections, unremitting vaginal yeast infections, and side effects of medications. Then there's the really serious stuff—meningitis, TB, pneumonia, blindness.

It is little wonder that patients with HIV were often interested in spiritual issues. Many wanted God's help to cope. Some wanted God's help in sorting through their guilt for getting themselves into their situation. Nearly all eventually wanted assurance that the next life would offer something better.

I met Meriediana in the hospital room of her common-law husband, Frederico, along with their ten-year-old daughter. Dr. Moore had cared for her husband since he became sick and had occasionally talked with him about God's love. A month or two before his death, Frederico had opened his heart to receive that love. As part of his new Christian commitment, he asked Dr. Moore's pastor to marry him and Meriediana in his hospital room. He died a couple of weeks later quite at peace, moments before I came into his room on rounds.

Meriediana didn't understand the source of his peace. The *santeria*[41] she had practiced for fifteen years was all the religion she wanted. Furthermore, she didn't understand enough English to read the HIV prevention brochures. She certainly didn't understand Dr. Moore when he told her a few weeks later that her own blood tested positive for HIV. She felt fine. How could she have the virus?

Meriediana kept coming to Esperanza Health Center irregularly over the next five years. She didn't understand why she should take the prescribed medicine, though she gradually realized that her nurse and her doctors really cared about her. Whether she had physical problems or family problems, their gentle words and hugs meant a lot. She liked it when they prayed for her, even if she didn't understand all they said.

Despite this care, her anger at having HIV infection grew. Little by little she began hearing voices telling her to kill her daughter, herself, and sometimes other people. When the voices told her to stop taking her medicines, her immunity sank, and with it her weight and her blood count. She finally was admitted to a psychiatric hospital, little more than a skeleton, with behavior out of control, hair fallen out, and an anemia so severe that she could hardly walk.

One night in the hospital she had a vision of a huge, shining angel and of a dove landing on her bed. She awoke with a clear mind for the first time in weeks, convinced that she should be a Christian and not practice *santeria* any longer. She was discharged a short time later, and rapidly improved. Our staff wondered if she would relapse when her mother died a year later. We were amazed at her peace and strength during that ordeal. When I saw her three weeks after her mother's death, she looked radiantly healthy, with regained weight, hair, red blood count, and immunity. She assured me she had no more crazy thoughts. When I asked what caused her to get better, she answered quickly, "God! Only God could have helped me this much! And the Esperanza staff. They have been like family. They are the best family I have!"

Esperanza's combination of medical care, emotional care, and spiritual care proved life-changing for Charlotte as well.

---

[41] *Santeria* is a mixture of herbal medicine, spiritualism, and Catholicism.

Charlotte was raped by a family friend when she was about six years old. Because he threatened to kill her family if she told anyone, she kept quiet about the incident. When she was ten, an uncle repeated the violation. This time she told her mom, only to hear, "You wanted that to happen!" Another uncle raped her a third time at age thirteen with the warning, "If you tell your mom, she will just think you are some kind of a whore." She felt her mom already believed this. Frequent beatings from both parents discouraged her from reporting it to anyone. Not until the Department of Human Services threatened to put her in a foster home did the beatings stop—when she was sixteen.

By then, she was looking for love in other places. She had her first daughter at seventeen. A couple of years later, a second man gave her a son—and Chlamydia and gonorrhea. Desperate for love, she stayed with him through another pregnancy. When he saw that the new baby was not a boy, he stomped out of the delivery room and never came back. Heartbroken, she eventually turned to a third young man. She was nearly suicidal and hardly cared whether she contracted a disease. She also realized he would refuse to have sex with her if she insisted they use a condom. She could not handle any more rejection. Later, he joked with her, "Hey, guess what? I have AIDS!"

Pregnant again, she went to a clinic across town for routine prenatal care. There, to her shock, she discovered that he hadn't been joking. *She now had HIV.*

And having HIV, she was branded, "one of *those* people." She cringed to see that "HIV+" was already stamped on the cover of her chart. When she walked out of the exam room, she heard nurses whispering to the doctor, "Did you tell her? Did you tell her?" *Why was it everybody's business?* she wondered angrily. She stayed at that clinic for the duration of her pregnancy, but she began looking for another source of health care.

The respect and confidentiality with which she was treated at Esperanza impressed her immediately. She wasn't particularly interested in spiritual issues. Nonetheless, Dr. Hollinger and Missy, her nurse, began to tell her about God's love for her and sometimes to pray with her. She and Missy had many long conversations about what she thought of herself, her relationship with her fiancé, and how God could heal the brokenness she felt so deeply. She shared some of her reflections with me.

"It was really kind of funny to see a clinic that talks about God so much. And I couldn't believe it. And when I met Missy, there was just

something that I loved about her. And then when she started talking about God, I noticed that it was through God that let her have that type of attitude. And I just started to see how God works in people. And I started to say to myself, I said, you know, even though I am going through a tremendous thing, I believe that God can make me into a new person. And I don't have to feel so dirty and so not wanted. I believe that God would actually want me, and I wouldn't have to have sex with him."

Charlotte began attending church with Missy. Seeing a change in her, her fiancé decided to come also. A few weeks later, at the church of Charlotte's uncle and aunt, both had their first experience with God. Charlotte described it to me.

It was such a good feeling! I felt like a new person. I felt like a cold wave over my body. Ever since, I go around smiling, and people say, "What's wrong with you? "Like the Bible says, "old things are passed away, all things are become new!" And I feel that way!"

With such spiritual encouragement, Charlotte began taking her medicines faithfully and followed through on other medical recommendations. Gradually she began to think about herself and her life differently.

The pastor of my church, he let us know that you're not alone in this world, even though you feel like you are, that God is able to take that disease out of your body—yeah, he knows—and the pastor, he doesn't treat me any different even knowing that he knows. He treats me just like anybody else...You know, even knowing that I know all these things, the devil still puts in my head that, you know, you was out there, and you was doing your own thing. 'Cause I was out there, not thinking about the consequences, sleeping with this guy, sleeping with that guy. I still sometimes feel like I'm nothing, but I know that with Jesus Christ I am everything.

She and her fiancé decided not to have sex anymore, with or without condoms, till they were married. Then they would trust God to keep their condoms from breaking. Her new baby, to her great joy, turned out to be HIV negative. Apart from sinus headaches, she had remained healthy as of my last contact with her.

◆　◆　◆　◆　◆　◆　◆

Not all of our patients did so well physically. Prior to the advent of highly-active antiretroviral treatments in March of 1996, we had no good way of stopping the virus. Patients would respond for perhaps six or twelve months to the single or double drug regimes that were available, and then once again resume their slide toward immune deficiency. For a couple of years we lost, on the average, one patient a month.

Usually, by the time a patient died, we had walked with him or her for several years through physical and emotional problems, family problems, legal problems, housing problems, and financial problems, not to mention drug problems. When you suffer with someone, you bond with him or her. We developed relationships with most patients that were deeply meaningful on both ends, completely apart from the medical aspects.

In the context of those relationships, it became particularly natural to talk about spiritual issues, often at our patients' initiative. How can one suffer and not wonder about the meaning of suffering, one's own responsibility for one's choices, the meaning of life, and the question of life hereafter? It was impossible not to share with these friends the hope that God had given us. Little by little, most of them responded, gradually opening their hearts to God's work. Now they were not only our patients and friends, but they were our brothers and sisters as well.

The goodbyes became a strange mixture of grief and joy. We were losing, and really missing, people who had become very dear to us. It was terribly painful. On the other hand, often God had somehow turned around this horrendous plague and made it the very instrument to bring them to Himself and to a quality of life and wholeness they had never experienced before. Without AIDS, they might have continued in their self-destructive lifestyles all the way into eternity. Thanks to AIDS, they would now live forever. We would see them again, this time vibrantly healthy and happy.

Arnaldo was diagnosed with HIV infection in his twenties. His years on Philadelphia's streets had taught him that, to survive, you had to beat the system or be beaten by it. He came to Esperanza gruff, dominating, adamant about everything, and determined to be in charge of his own care.

In the months following his diagnosis, his immune system deteriorated rapidly. We put him in the hospital because of a serious fungal infection in his esophagus. There, if the hospital staff didn't respond quickly to his ring, if his roommate didn't get his lunch tray, or if the room just didn't meet his expectations, he would scold or threaten the offender. Sometimes he would call the nursing supervisor from his room telephone. Arnaldo was a master of manipulation. He would talk sweetly to some staff to gain their favor and then pit them against other unsuspecting staff members.

As his health continued to deteriorate, Arnaldo would often threaten to find a "good" doctor somewhere else. Once while suffering from a high fever from three simultaneous infections, he phoned his mother to ask her to take him home, despite our pleading. Two days later he returned, sicker than ever.

Underneath the bravado, we occasionally saw a scared little boy who knew his life was out of control and who was terrified of dying. During those times Arnaldo eagerly received our explanations of God's love, and our prayers that God would work in his body and heart.

With the help of a local hospice, Arnaldo finally went home to the care of his mother. Dr. Hollinger continued visiting regularly to direct his medical care. His mom, a steadfast Christian, arranged for her small congregation to hold services in their modest sitting room. One Sunday afternoon while talking with her pastor, Arnaldo surrendered his life to God. Dr. Hollinger and the hospice nurses noticed a real change in his demeanor in the two weeks that followed. Arnaldo's sharp bristles seemed to have melded into a peace, a gentleness, even a thankfulness. One day, though he had become so weak he could barely talk, Arnaldo shouted after Dr. Hollinger as he left his bedroom, *"Dios te bendiga!"* (God bless you!). The next day he slipped into eternity.

◆　◆　◆　◆　◆　◆　◆

When Esperanza started, I didn't dream that Meriediana, Charlotte, Arnaldo, and others with AIDS would become my favorite patients. I discovered, not very originally, that love is its own reward. To see God at work in them added another dimension of remuneration. It is no exaggeration to say most of the AIDS patients we treated for any length of time had made peace with God before they died. Many who lived, despite their ups and downs, had also started new lives as a result of spiritual choices they made in response to their diagnosis. That I was then able, by good medical care, to help them live more comfortably and more normally only added to my job satisfaction.

In the spring of 1996, AIDS became a different disease. The new treatments available in the United States permitted many patients to achieve undetectable levels of virus in their blood stream and to recover much of their immunity. They felt better. They were almost never in the hospital.

We would learn, however, that the magic medicines are themselves poisons which can cause diabetes, liver damage, kidney stones, and other health problems. Too many patients took the medicines incorrectly and then developed resistance to one medicine after another. We watched the number of new infections each year rise across the country because of complacency and carelessness—byproducts, in a way, of the improved treatments. It was particularly painful to find that some of our newly infected patients were already resistant to new medicines—sure evidence that they had contracted the infection from someone who knew their diagnosis but who didn't bother to take precautions to protect others.

The medicines certainly hadn't solved the AIDS problem. It was far more than a medical problem. AIDS was a magnifying glass exposing the inequities, lack of interpersonal respect, selfishness, and despair that lies deep within the fabric of society. And we became increasingly aware that, bad as AIDS was in our neighborhood, it was causing almost unimaginable disaster in other parts of the world.

But wasn't the Church supposed to address topics like justice, respect, compassion, and hope? What if Christians could grasp that Jesus spent as much time healing bodies as saving souls? What if Christians really understood that He wanted to bring God's reign to every aspect of society? What if they began tackling some of the root causes of AIDS? What if Christians began recalling their own sins enough to stop judging people with AIDS, and began loving them—toughly when necessary, but unconditionally? What if church people would lay aside ignorant phobias and offer the hugs and touches that people with AIDS so need? What if preachers who forever harangued about "evangelism" would encourage their congregations to get involved with persons with HIV disease? What if we even made AIDS a priority in our charitable giving, as the gay community and so many others had done?

I was beginning to hear that Uganda was turning around its AIDS epidemic. Churches and mosques were playing a major role in that process. Future research would demonstrate that millions of people really changed their sexual behavior, and not just by using more condoms.[42] In the view of secular agencies, that was a miracle.

Well, what if the Church would pray *"Thy Kingdom come, Thy will be done on earth as it is in heaven,"* in regards to the AIDS epidemic? I didn't imagine there was any AIDS in heaven. Then what if, around the world, the Church would take responsibility for helping to answer that prayer? The miracle of Uganda would happen in other places as well. Now that would be a miracle, for sure – one that might convince a lot of unbelievers of the reality of God.

We didn't, however, need to wait for that day to see miracles....

---

[42] *Rethinking AIDS Prevention,* by Edward C. Green, Praeger Publishers, Westport, Connecticut; 2003.

Miracles

"Hey, how's this for news?" Ron handed me the new *Time Magazine* as he sat down to breakfast.

The headline of the cover story announced, "Can Prayer, Faith, and Spirituality Really Improve Your Physical Health? A Growing and Surprising Body of Scientific Evidence Says They Can."[43]

"Not bad," I grinned at him. I had just seen *Newsweek's* counterpart, a cover story on faith healing, the week before. I skimmed the *Time* article while I munched my cereal. It was an amazingly favorable review of the mounting evidence that healthy spirituality extends life, speeds healing after surgery, improves function in chronic illness, decreases mental illness, helps break addictions, and increases quality of life. "Looks like we're making the big time!" I giggled, kissing him goodbye.

Two hours later, as I sat down to tackle some paperwork, the phone rang. "Hello, this is Fox TV. We were referred to you by the Christian Medical and Dental Society. We're doing a story on miracles and medicine. Could we talk to you about your experiences with faith and healing?"

What a wonderful opportunity to give God some long overdue credit! We agreed to meet at Esperanza at 3:00 that afternoon. I buzzed the front desk to warn them to expect a television crew.

◆　◆　◆　◆　◆　◆　◆

Quickly I pushed aside the stacks on my desk and grabbed a piece of scratch paper. What kinds of miracles of healing *had* I seen?

First and most obviously, there were *medical miracles*—times when God seemed to give extraordinary wisdom to doctors. I remembered the mysterious illness that swept through a drug rehab center, threatening the life of one staff member and incapacitating several others. Eventually shrewd detective work by Dr. Mike Moore and others pieced together the puzzle.

---

[43] *Time Magazine,* June 24, 1996.

Or was it God who had helped them ferret out the fact that some pet birds in the center's aviary were not well? They had psittacosis, a disease common among birds though rare in humans. Once the cause was clear, everybody got treated and promptly got well.

And I would never forget the Sunday morning that Dr. Moore kept Juan DeJesus alive when all his other hospital docs, including me, had given up. Mike was not on call, but I thought I owed it to him to let him know his friend Juan had "crashed" with *Pneumocystis carinii* pneumonia and probably would not live more than a few hours. To my surprise, Mike sent his family to church and came in to the ICU. He spent the entire day hovering over Juan, adjusting medicines and titrating the IV fluids against his lung findings practically moment by moment. Juan miraculously pulled through not only that day, but for the next two months.

Eduardo had needed a different type of miracle – a miracle of provision. Eduardo had been discharged from the hospital, recovered from the fungal meningitis that had almost killed him, but dependent on the anti-fungal drug, Diflucan, for the rest of his life. Diflucan was about $4.00 per tablet, and Eduardo had little money, no health insurance, and no eligibility for assistance. That very afternoon, knowing none of this, the drug rep from Pfizer walked into Esperanza with more than a thousand dollars' worth of Diflucan under his arms, samples he was glad to see Eduardo use. I hadn't known angels dressed as drug reps!

On a third level, we routinely saw miracles of emotional healing at Esperanza. Rosemary came to Esperanza depressed and nearly suicidal. She had been abused as a child and was at that time abusing her own children. She had received secular counseling and medication for years, without benefit. At Esperanza, in addition to giving her standard medications and counseling, her doctor began explaining that God loved her and wanted to forgive and help her. Gradually her hostility toward God melted away. Eventually she prayed in one of our exam rooms, asking God to come into her life. Over the next days, weeks, and months, we saw her depression lift and her behavior improve dramatically. What if we had only given her Prozac?

Sometimes I had seen emotional healing result in dramatic physical healing. I remembered Rose, whose excruciating migraine disappeared instantly when she opened herself to God's love. And Mary, whose severe asthma completely cleared seconds after we prayed together about some deep hurts she had experienced. And Myra, whose stomach pain vanished as she began to trust God with a difficult relational problem.

Some people needed more than emotional healing. Only *permanent lifestyle changes* could cure many types of medical problems. Yet many patients seemed to hang onto their health-destroying habits despite our best information and advice, the latest in behavior modification techniques, and even the pain of serious consequences. I'd seen drug addicts make dramatic behavior changes as they were coming to know God. But other people, with diabetes and heart disease and emphysema, needed similar miracles.

For example, my friend Susan grew up with more than her share of pain. Her father had sexually abused her. Her brother disappeared without explanation or trace. During her first two marriages, which were disasters, she turned to cigarettes: they, at least, would always be there for her.

Her third husband, Bill, was wonderful. Motherhood, however, proved to be a struggle. Alone without mentor or support while Bill was at work, she began turning also to the refrigerator for solace. A trim 128 pounds at that time, Susan exactly doubled her weight over the next eighteen years.

Susan knew she needed to stop smoking. She tried every stop-smoking program she ever heard of, but she always relapsed within a few months. Even holding her mother in her arms as she died of lung cancer did nothing to break her own tobacco habit. One night, thirty years into her smoking addiction and sick with bronchitis, she became desperate. Hurling her cigarette into the sink, she cried out loud, "Oh God, *please* let me stop this! I cannot stop it by myself! Please help me!" When she awoke the next morning, she realized she had no craving for cigarettes. In the ten years since then, she has never smoked again.

However, her weight remained a problem. It was all too easy to seek comfort in chocolate and other delicacies. And she needed comfort, in big doses. Sometimes the pain from all the trauma of her past washed over her in waves. Sometimes the realities of the present almost crushed her. Her son, who had been sexually abused in a park when he was twelve, was now wrestling with self-mutilating impulses. Her sister, her only living relative, was serving time for stealing Susan's identity—using her credit card, taking out loans in Susan's name. Susan dreaded every time the phone would ring. What new disaster would await her? The pain in her soul was so intense that she found herself wishing she could just die. She knew her blood pressure was dangerously high, driven up not only by stress, but also by her weight. Secretly she hoped for a stroke so big that she wouldn't linger in a nursing home.

She also had pain in her body. Her excess weight caused the arthritis in her knees to become intolerable, forcing her to give up her job as a nurse. Breast cancer, another disease correlated with obesity, plunged her into the miseries of surgery and radiation. Even her gall bladder was acting up, as commonly happens in overweight people. Still she continued to put on pounds, though she had tried every commercial weight-loss program she could find.

One day during a gall-bladder attack, Susan again cried out, "God, you've got to help me! This has got to stop, and I don't know how to stop it! I'm going to kill myself if I keep eating like this!"

She reported to me afterward that something changed in her brain that day. She found herself wanting to live, to grow old with her husband, to be able to make some contribution to the world. What happened to her son was between him and God; she could not kill herself over him. She found herself choosing to be healthy, over and over. "I don't *want* that donut; it's going to kill me," she began telling herself. "I'm going to eat right and exercise more. And I'm not doing it because I want to be sexy and get some guy. Bill is not going to love me more if I lose weight. This is for me!"

What happened to Susan went far deeper than her fat cells. She started believing that God loved her when she had been doing some really bad things, that He loved her now, and that after what He had done for her on Calvary, there was no way He could love her more. She didn't want to dishonor Him any longer by destroying His creation—herself. So when Bill would get ice cream before bedtime, she would reach for an apple. She did not diet or join any program. But the weight came off, about a pound a week—64 pounds at last count. Without medication, her blood pressure returned completely to normal. And her arthritis pain was lessening.

If only I could help all of my obese patients to find what Susan had found!

Finally, there were also *purely supernatural miracles*, completely unexplainable by medical science.

I remembered an old man whose esophageal carcinoma had simply vanished over a week. I had viewed the biopsy slides myself, and there was no doubt about the diagnosis. But the gastroenterologist wanted some additional photos, and the patient graciously permitted another esophagoscopy. For two hours they had run up and down his esophagus, searching in vain for the mass they had seen the week before. It didn't show up on a barium swallow, either. Afterwards he admitted to me that his church was praying for him. A year later, when I saw him for another condition, he had had no trace of recurrence.

I also remembered the night two years before when I sent Miguel to the emergency room. Miguel was an AIDS patient who had come to know the Lord and really cleaned up his life. He had been getting sick for several days, but he had refused to go to the hospital until he finished fixing his leaking roof. He didn't want to leave his wife alone in that house with rain threatening. By that afternoon he could hardly climb down the ladder. He reported fever and chills, a profound weakness, a painful cough, shortness of breath, and foul-smelling phlegm. I was pretty sure he had a bacterial pneumonia. I asked the ER physician to call me after he evaluated Miguel. Then, bushed, I went home and toppled into bed with my beeper on my nightstand. About 6:00 the next morning I awoke, a bit panicked that the ER doctor had not called me. "Oh, we were pretty busy, and I didn't get to see him until about 9:00. By then he was fine, and the chest x-ray done around 11:00 was clear. So I sent him home." As soon as I got to work, I called Miguel. He was indeed fine. His church started praying for him around 7 the night before, about the time he suddenly began feeling better.

I looked over my notes. Yes, I could do a good job of talking about faith-based healings. They certainly didn't happen all the time; at least we couldn't produce them on demand. Maybe I would never understand why God would heal one person and not another who had prayed just as hard. Perhaps spiritual warfare was real, and we had not yet finished defeating the enemy. But there was no doubt that miracles do sometimes happen. God certainly had given us enough examples.

I laid aside my notes and began to tackle the more mundane papers on my desk.

◆ ◆ ◆ ◆ ◆ ◆ ◆

At 3:00, the TV crew arrived. I greeted them in the waiting room and invited them to my office. As soon as they set their stuff down, the young woman asked, "Where's the patient?"

"The patient? I thought you wanted to interview me!" I rejoined.

"Oh no, we always like to interview actual cases."

Blushing to the tips of my ears, I returned, "Of course. I'll get a patient in here right away!"

While they set up their lights in the exam room across the hall from my office, I flew to the phone. I couldn't find a phone number for Eduardo. Rosemary was at work across town. Mary was out of state. Rose was not home. Myra couldn't leave her job. Susan was in the next county. I had no idea how to reach the old man. Miguel had died tragically a few months before of an unusual side effect of a medication.

I returned to the hallway to answer a question from the camera person. As we conferred, Dr. Hollinger tapped me on the shoulder. "If you want someone to interview, I think I have just the person for you!"

"Who?" I lifted my eyebrows.

"Brenda Ramos![44] You wouldn't believe what just happened!"

I remembered Brenda, a beautiful young woman in her 20's. Dr. Hollinger had treated her for months for a debilitating condition called tardive dyskinesia, a rare but serious complication of a medicine she was taking for her nerves. She had developed uncontrollable tongue thrusting and contortions of her face and mouth, made worse by attempts to talk. She carried a towel everywhere she went, to catch the saliva constantly dripping from her mouth and also to hide her contorted face from public view. In her early days at Esperanza, her speech could be understood with difficulty, but recently she could manage only inarticulate grunts. She carried a note-pad to communicate. Because of the severity of her condition, she had dropped out of college, despairing of ever being able to work.

Dr. Hollinger had consulted a psychiatrist/neurologist with years of experience with tardive dyskinesia, but no medical regime brought relief. The psychiatrist confirmed that even when tardive dyskinesia does improve, it takes months to go away. On the other hand, in 50% of cases it never improves. After eight months of treatment without improvement, the psychiatrist had prepared to send her to the National Institutes of Health in Washington, D.C., hoping Brenda might benefit from some experimental medication there.

---

[43] The details of this true story of Brenda Ramos, whose real name is used here, are taken from articles published in *Health and Development*, vol 4, p.3-8, 1997. Dr. Bryan Hollinger's article is called "Bigger Prayers to a Bigger God." Brenda Ramos's article, as told to Helen Grace Lescheid, is called "The Hem of His Cloak."

About fifteen minutes previously, Dr. Hollinger had been standing in the hallway charting on a patient he had just seen. He glanced into the waiting room, where Brenda and her mother were waiting for him without an appointment. He nodded a hello and returned to his charting.

"Hi, Dr. Hollinger!" It was Brenda's voice, clear and without distortion.

He dropped his pen in disbelief and sprinted into the waiting room. He grilled her with questions; she gave perfectly clear replies. He watched fearfully—expecting any moment to see her tongue jab out mercilessly and her face twist in spasm—but there wasn't even the slightest twitch.

Had she begun taking a new medicine? No.

Had she discontinued any old medications? No.

When he calmed down, she told him her story. About ten days previously, she had become so discouraged she felt she couldn't bear to live any longer. In desperation, she and her mother had prayed almost ceaselessly for three days and nights, pleading with God to deliver her from this condition. Unknown to them, Brenda's brother was fasting and praying also. The second day, Brenda's mother thought Brenda was speaking a bit more clearly but was afraid to say anything for fear of raising false hopes. Then over the next two days, her symptoms disappeared completely. She waited a few days before telling Dr. Hollinger, just to make sure, but had decided this afternoon that she couldn't wait any longer!

I ran to the waiting room ahead of Bryan. Brenda smiled at me and quickly—and clearly—agreed to be interviewed on camera.

That night Brenda's testimony of God's healing power went out on FOX TV across the nation. My brother saw it in San Diego and called my parents to tell them about it. That night I added to my list, *"miracles of timing."*

Hope Even for Me

12

Even from a half block away I could see that Ron was furious. He and David, bats and batting helmets slung over their shoulders, had already walked halfway to the subway. I was supposed to pick them up after the little league game at 6:15. It was now after 7:00. I pulled the car over to the curb and threw open the passenger doors. I smiled my most conciliatory smile.

"I'm really sorry, dear. I know there's no excuse for my being late."

"Then when are you going to change? You're always sorry, but you never change!"

Clearly it would do no good to explain that Andrea, our jewel of a head nurse, had plopped herself down in my office after the other nurses had gone to unload her day's frustrations. Andrea, of all people, must not be allowed to burn out. She was far too valuable to Esperanza and to us all. Nor could I communicate why I had taken twenty minutes after she finally left to straighten my desk. A little island of slight order in the midst of the chaos of my office would help me face tomorrow.

Nonetheless, Ron was right. This sort of thing was happening fairly frequently. Only last night I had called from the hospital to say I had a patient to admit, but I should be home by 7:15. Ron had decided to wait dinner on me, because he and David and I had precious little time together these days.

But the case of Arnaldo, an AIDS patient whose esophageal fungal infection was resisting the usual antibiotics, was complicated. I had written my usual very complete admissions note, hoping to raise his chances of getting good care from the other hospital staff. With secret pleasure, I remembered a comment one senior resident doctor had made a few weeks previously. "You and Dr. Hollinger and Dr. Nieves are some of the best attending physicians we have here. You do far more thorough admissions notes than most others do." I also took a little extra time to talk and pray with Arnaldo. He seemed calmer when I left. More than one of my patients had told me over the years that I was the best doctor they ever had. Something in me wanted all of my patients to feel that way.

I arrived home at 8:45. Both of my guys had eaten peanut butter and jelly sandwiches. David was asleep.

There also was the matter of Leo. Esperanza had been without an executive director for two months. Ted Hewson, Esperanza's administrator, and I had picked up the slack as best we could. It was a miracle that Leo Treviño, a bright young Latino from New York, had accepted the job—even after we showed him Esperanza's precarious financial condition.. Leo had been on board for a month now. He quickly gained respect from the staff and board, and he was improving community relations daily. Still, he was new and couldn't be expected to pick up on everything all at once. During the transition, his newness seemed to justify my working sixty-five to seventy hours a week.

I promised Ron I would level with my counselor, Jim Petty, at my four o'clock appointment the next day.

◆　◆　◆　◆　◆　◆　◆

I had been seeing Jim off-and-on for five years for help with my workaholism. At first I went just to please my husband. Soon, however, I realized I really had a problem, and it went deep inside me. Though very sympathetic with the work of Esperanza, Jim had helped me over the years make a number of changes to preserve my health, sanity, and marriage. Unfortunately, I somehow always managed to subvert our best plans and end up in the old behavior patterns.

On the day of my appointment, I didn't manage to leave work until 3:30. I ran several dark yellow lights and made some spectacular horn-honking passes, trying to compress the forty-minute drive to Jim's office. I still walked in late.

"Your workaholic is in full relapse again," I confessed, perhaps to make my tardiness seem more excusable.

I reported to Jim the number of hours I had worked, as I always did. Then I described the scenes of the last two nights.

"So how do you feel about it this time?" he parried.

"Guilty, as usual." I could hardly remember not feeling guilty about one area of my life or another. As soon as I wrestled one area under control, another would display my inadequacies for the world to see.

"No, I mean, how are you really, inside?"

I hated that kind of question. It was so much easier not to think, not to feel. I performed pretty well most of the time. I was—except for a few gaffes now and then—a good wife, a good mother, a good Christian. If I played the role well enough, hopefully Ron wouldn't notice the lack of feeling that I had for him—or for anything. God probably *had* noticed my lack of feeling for Him, but He hadn't struck me dead yet. And He still pretty regularly answered my daily prayers for help.

Nonetheless, I knew I was in trouble. The past week, my inability to think of familiar medication names and dosages had embarrassed me in front of a medical student rotating through Esperanza. I had actually spelled my name wrong on a prescription. I had shot up urgent mini-prayers that I wouldn't do something really stupid and hurt a patient. So far I hadn't—but when would it happen?

And my right hip was really starting to hurt. I had experienced periodic joint pain for a couple of years, usually when I was not getting enough sleep. Today, for the first time, I had actually limped into Jim's office.

"Wasn't there a guy named Jacob whose hip got knocked out of joint wrestling with an angel?" Jim quipped. We both laughed.

Then he turned to me in dead seriousness and pronounced, "Carolyn, you need to quit Esperanza, and you need to quit now."

I was shocked. Jim had never talked to me like that. I argued fiercely. Surely there was another solution. This was just a temporary crisis, and Esperanza still was not ready to do without me.

Jim remained adamant. "If you have a problem with alcohol, you should not work at a bar!"

◆　◆　◆　◆　◆　◆　◆

That night Ron and I talked about what Jim had said. We concluded that his prescription was a little more radical than necessary. All I really needed was eight hours sleep each night and time with God every morning to get my head together. This week we would make sure that I obtained these.

The next day our son, David, and his friend were mugged on the way home from school. The evening was shot waiting at the police station for the officer to take our report.

The following day I came home to find the international student living with us in tears over an impending music theory exam. I sat with her at the piano, and we worked through chord progressions until 10:30 p.m.

Not one night that week did I get anything close to eight hours of sleep. Not one morning did I have a relaxed time with God. By Friday I was nearly brain dead. Just after noon, Dr. Hollinger popped into my office and asked me to come and take a look at a patient's rash. We always helped one another with unusual rashes. I looked up at him and whispered, "Bryan, I can't! I just don't have it!"

He looked hard at me, and then told me I'd better go home.

Saturday evening Ron and I had dinner with Ron and Arbutus Sider, dear friends with whom we had met regularly for years. Eventually the conversation came around to how I was. I replied honestly about what the last couple of weeks had been like. Immediately Ron and Arbutus responded, "You need to take a week off!" My Ron joined them.

"You've got to be kidding!" I retorted. "You mean, I'm supposed to call in tomorrow and say I'm going to be sick for a week?" Anyone who would dare to pull that stunt with me would receive my contempt.

"Exactly!" They all affirmed, practically in unison.

I could not argue that they didn't understand. They knew the needs of Esperanza almost as well as I did. They also loved me. I realized I had to listen. Sunday night I called Leo and told him I was taking the week off. He responded graciously. He reminded me that a resident doctor would be rotating through and could see most of my patients.

◆　◆　◆　◆　◆　◆　◆

It was Easter week. David was out of school. He and I puttered around the house and made puppets for his class project. I skipped his little league games, church, and everything else that would raise my adrenaline level. I slept for hours. By Saturday night I was thinking clearly, feeling emotion again, and free from hip pain.

After David was in bed, Ron and I discussed the implications of our experiment. My diagnosis was no longer in question. I was in danger of becoming like one of my drug addicts, checking into a detox program to get the habit down to an affordable level, then going back to the streets to use again. Was I serious about changing?

We looked at different options. Perhaps I could work part time. Perhaps I could stop seeing patients for a while and just administrate. I knew, though, that administration was an open pit with no bottom. Perhaps I could just see patients. That would not work either. As long as I was at Esperanza, people would turn to me for answers to administrative questions. Ron and I both realized that, however we set it up, I would sooner or later subvert whatever safeguards we tried to build in. Furthermore, our family could not live on a part-time Esperanza salary and still keep our daughter in college. It hurt to admit it, but Jim was right. I would have to leave Esperanza.

Hoping yet for a way out, the next morning I asked the elders of my church for special prayer after the service. They were into missions. Surely they would be concerned for Esperanza's future. Briefly I described the situation.

They quickly concurred with our decision. "You need to lay Esperanza down, Carolyn. It's God's project, not yours," my pastor gently exhorted. Then they prayed that God would strengthen me to do what I needed to do.

◆　◆　◆　◆　◆　◆　◆

That afternoon I cried. At first I cried in self pity. Then, little by little, I realized I had bigger things to cry about. I had treated God as if He could not possibly run His kingdom without me. I had acted as if neither His compassion nor His memory were all that great. In fact, I might have to pick up after Him where He dropped the ball. That was a huge insult to God, who had arranged history so as to give His Son's life for me. If He had feelings, and I had no reason to believe they were deadened because *He* overworked, then I must have hurt Him dreadfully. It dawned on me that nothing I could *do for* Him would impress Him, so long as I was not *relating to* Him appropriately.

I realized something else. It was not love that I had been seeking through my drivenness. To be loved unconditionally is not a great compliment to one's ego. No, I wanted people to admire me, to think I was wonderful, to honor me. I wanted to be superior, even though I preached that everyone was equal before God. If I was better than the rest of mankind, I would not have to depend on God—or anyone else—for my sense of worth.

Of course, I would never have admitted this, and perhaps had not even been fully conscious of it. I had often made self-effacing statements. I had tried to make even my humility superior to everyone else's. How hypocritical I had been. It was not a pretty realization.

Then I saw how this pride had led to me to patronize those I believed inferior to me; even to feel a secret contempt for those "less enlightened." I had hurt those with whom I lived and worked. I was more intent on proving my own adequacy in every situation than on listening and adapting to their real needs.

If I had pushed people away by my pride, I had done so even more with God. I recalled the story of Adam and Eve – how their desire for independence from God prompted them to violate the terms of their intimacy with Him. What they did, viewed from the perspective of what they lost, was tragic, stupid, ugly. I shuddered to see the same dynamics at work within me.

That afternoon I finally felt sorry, and not just because I had gotten caught. I faced the root causes of my workaholism. For once I hated my distrust of everyone but myself, my glory-hogging, my exalted self-importance. I stood before God empty-handed. I found Him waiting for me—waiting for me to put down my heavy load so He could take me in His arms. My tears became tears of relief, tears of a small child at last safe in a father's embrace. That night I slept peacefully and dreamlessly.

◆ ◆ ◆ ◆ ◆ ◆ ◆

I did not look forward to informing Leo and Ted of my impending departure. I felt like a lieutenant telling his captain in the heat of battle that he was deserting. We met Monday afternoon in Leo's office.

"I need to tell you brothers that I am resigning from Esperanza, effective June 30." Briefly I shared why. There was a long silence.

Leo was first to respond. "I'm surprised that this should happen now. On the other hand, I'm not too surprised. A couple of weeks ago I was awakened about 2:30 a.m. with a picture of Abraham laying his precious son Isaac on the altar of sacrifice. I felt as though God were saying to me that I needed to lay you [and another staff member] on the same altar and prepare to give you up!"

Although Ted had had no visions, he likewise released me.

We decided not to say anything yet to other staff. It was possible that we might connect with a doctor looking for a position like mine at the fifteenth annual Christian Community Health Fellowship conference the coming weekend. If a replacement were in sight, it would be a lot easier to break the news to the rest of the staff.

Leo, Dr. Bryan Hollinger, and I represented Esperanza at the conference in Cleveland. It was a good conference, as usual, but no job-hunting doctors surfaced.

About midway through the conference, I pulled Bryan aside.

"Bryan, I cannot keep this from you any longer. I'm leaving Esperanza at the end of June. I haven't managed my resources well, and I've used them all up. Now I have to abandon ship to get my act together. I'm really sorry. I've failed God and I've failed you and the gang. Would you please forgive me?"

"Of course I forgive you." He could say no more. We both cried. It had been my writings and speeches that attracted Bryan initially to consider coming to Esperanza. As a young doctor fresh out of residency, he had looked to me as a mentor and role model. Recently he and I had shared responsibility for the sickest of our HIV patients. We relied heavily on one another. He and his wife Judy were dear friends to Ron and me. Now, I was leaving him in the lurch.

◆   ◆   ◆   ◆   ◆   ◆   ◆

Monday morning dawned bright and clear in Philadelphia. One by one I asked senior staff members into my office and recited the bad news. Tears flowed several times, interspersed with waves of apprehension. Now that the conference was over with no new doctor appearing, where would Esperanza find my replacement?

Simple, we laughed tersely. We just have to put an ad in the paper:

WANTED: Seasoned physician, board certified or eligible, experienced in advanced HIV care, fluent in Spanish, skilled in medical administration, able to provide spiritual leadership, willing to relocate immediately to the most drug-infested neighborhood in Philadelphia, prepared to take a two-thirds salary cut.

If no replacement materialized, how would those who remained, stretched already, absorb my responsibilities? Could Esperanza survive without my leadership?

Between tears I saw patients, finished charts, wrote grant proposals, and answered phone calls. Ted was equally busy—so busy, in fact, that he did not get around to returning the call of a Dr. Gadea from western Pennsylvania until the next day.

When he did, we could hardly believe his story.

During his college days, Dr. Ramon Gadea, a native of Puerto Rico, had felt called to be a missionary. But first medical school, then residency and an infectious disease fellowship, and then a wife and two small children filled his life. He had settled into a small town in western Pennsylvania, where his services as a specialist in infectious disease were in demand in three hospitals. He had a lucrative contract with one hospital and had just bought a nice house. He had no thoughts of leaving.

About a month previously, Dr. Gadea had been driving between hospitals when he got a call on his car phone informing him that one of his AIDS patients had just died. He began to cry. Only a week before, he had talked extensively with that patient about his relationship with God. He did not know what decision the patient had made. He flipped on his car tape player to get some comfort. The next song on the tape was about "la esperanza" ("the hope"). Suddenly a thought flashed across his mind, "Call Esperanza Health Center!"

He dismissed it. He had never been to Esperanza and knew no one there. He had only heard of Esperanza from a *Physician Magazine* article he had clipped about three years before, and had driven by the center once with a friend. But the thought kept returning with increasing strength, and after a few weeks he looked for the article. Apparently it had been lost in a move. He tried to put it out of his mind, but he could not escape the feeling that he must call. Finally, he telephoned the publishers of *Physician* to get Esperanza's phone number. He did not know I had announced my resignation that very day.

Dr. Gadea was fascinated by Ted's description of who we were and what we were about. He had been handed an unexpected vacation the following week, complete with in-laws to baby-sit his children. He and his wife Amy flew to Philadelphia at their own expense to check us out.

At staff meeting that morning, each of the doctors told why we had come to Esperanza and what we were getting out of working there. Ramon and Amy shared their personal stories. We were all quite moved. We showed them Esperanza. We took them on a tour of the neighborhood, and of possible neighborhoods where they might like to live. They left that night impressed, but only admitting to maybe a ten percent chance that they might actually come.

As the weeks passed, coincidences kept pointing the Gadeas to inner city Philadelphia, just when they were ready to forget the whole thing. Late in May, Ramon and Amy returned, again at their own expense. This time the conversation was very serious. God had remarkably prepared Ramon to do my job. However, the obstacles to their coming were also serious. Amy's elderly parents were within commuting distance of their present home. A new home in Philly would be too far away for an easy visit. To say the least, Ramon would have difficulty getting out of the contract he had signed with his hospital.

We kept praying. They kept praying.

◆ ◆ ◆ ◆ ◆ ◆ ◆

Friday, June 28, arrived. I had limited time to say goodbye to my beloved comrades, because David broke his hand that afternoon and I had to rush across town to meet him at Children's Hospital. I returned on Saturday to clean out my desk. I faced the daunting task of sorting through memories and resources and junk accumulated over fifteen years. I was still in the office at five o'clock when the phone rang. It was Ramon.

"Carolyn, Amy and I have decided to move to Philadelphia so I can accept the position as Esperanza's medical director."

I sat back, stunned. We had not spent a single dollar recruiting him. Ramon was to prove more effective in some ways as medical director than I had been. So God can't run His kingdom without me, huh?

Three days later Ron received a call to pastor a church in Indiana. Ever since Esperanza had opened, Ron had been teaching only part-time so he could cover the home base while I worked. We both had felt for some time that he should get back into pastoral ministry. As we prayed, it seemed this was the position to which God was calling him. We had less than six weeks to buy a house there, prepare our house for selling, sort through twenty years of accumulated possessions, pack, get away for a week of badly needed family vacation, and move half-way across the country. What if I had not already left Esperanza?

On August 18, 1996, Ron and I stood in front of our new church as its elders laid hands on us and committed us to God for the job we were to do. My tears flowed freely. I wondered if anyone else had the depth of joy I felt. How completely I had been forgiven—of so much! Furthermore, God had begun the process of changing me in ways I could not change myself. He had lifted me out of the "bar" and planted me in the middle of Indiana cornfields, where even a workaholic like me would be less tempted. I would not need to work as a physician, at least for a while, and I would not have specific responsibilities in the church. Yet in my new role as a pastor's wife, God was giving me another chance to serve Him.

Remembering the shining faces of my drug addicts who had been in rehab for a few weeks, I sang that morning at the top of my lungs. The God who had delivered them was delivering me, too!

Hope in the Face of Death

"Now it came about when all the nation had finished crossing the Jordan, that the Lord spoke to Joshua, saying,…'Take up for yourselves twelve stones from here out of the middle of the Jordan, from the place where the priests' feet are standing firm, and carry them over with you, and lay them down in the lodging place where you will lodge tonight.…So shall these stones become a memorial to the sons of Israel forever."[45]

D r. Tom Terry's rich voice almost sang the words from the ancient story of Joshua. I loved it when he taught my Sunday school class in our new church in Indiana. A professor at nearby Bethel College, he extracted all kinds of insights and applications from the simplest of Bible stories. Perhaps this morning's passage had its own power. Or it could have been his vivid descriptions of the two-million-strong mob crossing a flooded river on dry ground. Whatever the reason, his point this Sunday hit me forcefully, almost from his first sentence.

As voices rose and fell in discussion, I found myself thinking about Philadelphia. Though I had no official connection with Esperanza anymore, I still felt united with those who labored there so bravely. Like Joshua and the Israelites, we at Esperanza had crossed a few rivers on dry ground. Just the previous week, in September of 1996, we had needed $80,000 to make it through the month. Yesterday, Bryan's e-mail reported how all $80,000 had come in on time, $50,000 of it through an unexpected grant from the Huston Foundation. I had lost track of how many times God had bailed out Esperanza financially, usually at the last minute. How tragic it would be if those clear signs of His presence and power were forgotten.

Financial miracles were just the beginning of God's provision. Perhaps even more significant were the people God had directed our way, often with little or no effort on our part.

---

[45] Joshua 4:1,3,7

I thought of Laura Layer, the pediatrician-turned-seminary-student who had approached us in 1991 about doing her thesis on combined medical and spiritual care. Along with Marialena and a woman from a local church, she had visited every home on the block behind the health center, offering medical referrals, social service, and spiritual help as needed. They had uncovered all kinds of problems, not the least of which was the open sewage ditch running behind the houses. The city had never gotten around to fixing it, but these three women got the sewage ditch covered. They also found ways to provide care for a bunch of sick kids. In the process, they hooked up several families with the local church. When the project was over, Laura started work at Esperanza for little more than half the minimal salary we offered the other docs—because, as she insisted, she as a single woman could live more simply than we married folk.

I thought of my former office mate, Melissa Nieves, who as a child had lived in Esperanza's neighborhood. As a bilingual family physician, she could have worked anywhere she wanted. She chose to work at Esperanza for far less than she could have earned elsewhere, so she could minister God's love to her own people. She was now completing her fourth year there.

I remembered Bryan Hollinger's first visit to Esperanza. Bryan was just finishing his Master's in Public Health in drug abuse, on top of two medical specialty board certifications. A tip from a friend brought him to us, and we clearly needed him. We just weren't sure Esperanza would keep its doors open long enough to hire him. As deadlines for other job offers approached, he decided to turn them all down and wait. Our money finally came through, and after eight weeks of intensive language training in Guatemala, he began work at our clinic the next fall. What a blessing he had been ever since.

My mind went down the hall to Andrea Daft, the gentle, self-giving nurse who had supervised our nursing department for years. Andrea scored number one in the entire nation on her pediatric nursing licensure exam. How did we deserve her?

Or Elizabeth Hernandez, or Neil Schroeder, or Billy Robinson, each of whom had poured out their lives for counseling clients? In crisis after crisis, we docs had leaned heavily on their skillful and godly help.

I thought of Fred Estrada, one of North Philadelphia's most respected pastors. First as president of our board and later as executive director, Fred pastored patients, staff, vendors, agency heads—any human beings within reach. Once during a phonathon, I heard him pray about a crisis in a donor's life, completely forgetting to ask for money. With a lump in my throat, I remembered how Fred had responded when Ron's and my car was stolen. Without my knowledge, Fred began making calls. Within days he found a Christian car dealer willing to donate a used station wagon to our family, exactly the sort we needed, simply because we were "in ministry." Fred was now chaplain of a major university hospital in Philadelphia, and I had heard he was caring for troubled administrators and patients alike.

Then there was Ted. I remembered the almost supernatural way I had met Ted Hewson at that 1982 conference, and the way he had catalyzed Esperanza's work from behind the scenes for all those years. A computer genius, he knew financial modeling, health care trends, HMO's, and strategic planning. He also knew how to pray. His faith and administrative skills had pulled Esperanza along over difficult terrain on many occasions.

My mind flitted over others. There was Leo, our new executive director, who left a great job in New York to join us last year. I thought of receptionist Leslie Ramos, medical assistant Gloria Rodriguez, and medical record librarian Nilsa Casiano, who had served and believed and stuck with Esperanza for years, whether or not their paychecks arrived on time. And Nancy Hansen, the dynamo who had poured unbelievable energy into raising money for Esperanza over the years....

◆　◆　◆　◆　◆　◆　◆

My reverie was cut short as my classmates began to stand up, stretch, and start small talk. I found myself waiting to speak to Dr. Terry. When he was at last free, I confided the thought that had engaged my mind.

"Thanks for your lesson. I think God used it to speak specifically to me today. I have seen more than my share of miracles in the little health center where I used to work, and I think God wants me to write a book preserving those memories for future generations."

"Great! Let me know when it's published!"

However, by that afternoon I had pushed the idea to the back of my mind. That couldn't *really* have been God speaking to me. I had written a few magazine articles, but never a book. What made me think I could do that? Furthermore, Esperanza was struggling financially. What if Esperanza went belly-up before I finished writing the book? Who would want to read—let alone publish—a book on a health center that died?

Besides, if Esperanza were in trouble, what I should really do was try to stir up some Indiana money for it. Some farmers around Goshen were doing very well financially. The recreational vehicle industry was also causing many people to prosper. I had raised funds successfully in Philadelphia. Maybe I could siphon off some of Goshen's abundance for Esperanza.

The next day I phoned Esperanza and requested some fundraising materials, including the beautiful video that TV news anchor Diane Allen had just done on the center. Then I started making appointments—with two well-to-do couples from church, with the Christian real estate agent who had sold us our house, with a Christian businessman, and with a Christian doctor. I even sent an information packet to a missions committee of a nearby Mennonite church that had funded USA projects.

My new friends were cordial and polite. They could see that Esperanza was indeed a wonderful project. But didn't Goshen have its own disadvantaged people who needed health care? Why should they send money to someplace as removed from them as Philadelphia?

When I got home from my last disappointing interview, I stared hard into the mirror. What had happened to the dynamic and convincing fundraiser who helped to bring in a half-million dollars a few years back? Or did God simply enable me to do a particular job He had assigned me at that time, so that my fundraising success was never really to *my* credit in the first place? I remembered my grandmother talking about working under "the anointing." Well, I certainly saw no evidence of "anointing" on my fundraising efforts here. I felt like Samson shorn. Maybe God was really serious about wanting me to rest.

◆　◆　◆　◆　◆　◆　◆

In early November, Leo would be presenting Esperanza's needs to an elite group of Christian philanthropists. That was good. Esperanza's financial picture was looking increasingly grave. For some reason, churches had decreased their contributions. A foundation that had supported Esperanza heavily and consistently had experienced an internal political change which would likely end their giving. Recent billing problems had reduced the income collected from patients.

Besides all that, the health care environment had changed drastically. First, welfare reform was cutting off Medicaid insurance for many of our patients, and most of them were now coming in for care at the lowest rung of our sliding fee scale.

Second, a few months back the Commonwealth of Pennsylvania had forced all of our Medicaid patients to join various health maintenance organizations. This managed health care, through which providers receive a flat fee per patient rather than per visit, worked well for relatively healthy people. Generally, however, our patients were quite a bit sicker than the average, thanks to the effects of abject poverty, drug addiction, AIDS, mental illness, and the like. I remembered Pedro, whose mental illness, drug abuse, AIDS dementia, and dabbling in the occult combined to make him very difficult to treat. One year he visited Esperanza seventy-one times—not always seeing a doctor, but always requiring time and energy of staff members. Now Bryan said Pedro was drug free, mentally and spiritually stable, and healthy, without detectable HIV in his blood. But treating him hadn't helped our bottom line.

A third change had affected doctors across the country. Under the new health care economics, most doctors were expected to see more patients per hour, despite increased paperwork. Many were finding it difficult to practice good medicine technically, let alone attend to mental and social needs of their patients. Most didn't even try to address spiritual needs, which we believed were often key to helping people get well. The doctors at Esperanza weren't about to ignore these needs. Each of us had sacrificed greatly so we could work in a place allowing us to do medicine as we believed it should be done. As much as possible we docs tried to refer those with mental, social, and spiritual needs to other staff or to neighborhood clergy or volunteers. Even so, we were averaging 20 minutes or more per patient. And that didn't rake in the cash.

(It was not until years later, when I zipped through five or six patients an hour in a suburban practice, that I understood why some board members thought we should be doing better. Those patients and ours were worlds apart.)

◆　◆　◆　◆　◆　◆　◆

In mid-December Leo and I had a long talk by phone. Funds for the December 15 payroll had come in the morning of December 15, but there was no money for other outstanding bills. That day the state approved malpractice reform, but that would not reduce our insurance premiums for months. Leo didn't seem to have a concrete plan other than to "trust God." I didn't blame him. I remembered the hours Ted and I had spent at his computer trying first one set of conditions, then another on the complicated spreadsheet he had created to model Esperanza's finances. We already had cut staff and overhead, and had boosted productivity as much as we could. No scenario looked promising.

Christmas reminded me of another era in which taxes were heavy, a pregnant refugee had to make a home in a stable, and thousands of babies were murdered. Into that world of terrible oppression a child had come to say, "God can be trusted." Did I believe Him?

Trusting God was not altogether a bad idea. December 30th's payroll funds arrived the morning of December 30. The same thing happened on January 15. Yet how long could this go on?

The middle of February, our son, David, caught strep throat. I put him to bed, gave him some Tylenol, and trotted to the pharmacy to pick up some penicillin. The pharmacist spent more time than usual poring over his computer. Finally he came back to the counter.

"I'm sorry, Mrs. Klaus, you'll have to pay cash. Your health insurance coverage seems to have been cancelled."

What? We had good health insurance! When I left Esperanza, they had agreed to keep us on their group policy if we sent them our share of the premiums. We had been paying them faithfully ever since we left.

As soon as I got home, I called Ted.

"Yes, Carolyn, I'm sorry to tell you," he replied. "We were not able to pay our insurance bill last month. It's really not good; Esther's child was hospitalized briefly last week and our insurance will not cover it. We hope to have that situation remedied by the end of this month. But please pray."

I wasn't mad, as I imagined other staff might be. But this was very heavy. I decided to begin looking for local health insurance coverage, though it would cost more. And I did pray. That night I pondered the ancient words from the Psalmist,

From my distress I called upon the Lord.
    The Lord answered me and set me in a large place.
The Lord is for me; I will not fear;
    What can man do to me?...

It is better to take refuge in the Lord than to trust in man.
It is better to take refuge in the lord than to trust in princes....[46]

Three days later, Leo let me know that Esperanza's board had decided to file bankruptcy on March 3 if God didn't intervene. Esperanza was more than $100,000 in debt, and there were no rescuers on the horizon. Steve Weaver, the board chairman, would send out one final public appeal, broadcasting the state of Esperanza's financial affairs. With little hope that it would do any good, the lawyers had already begun drawing up bankruptcy papers.

That night, I sat upright on the bed, wide-eyed, long after Ron was asleep. Could Esperanza's failure be partly my fault? Had I sown its seeds by not being the right kind of leader? I knew that at times I had gotten so emotionally involved in Esperanza's affairs, I couldn't pull back and see needs objectively. I knew I was miserable at estimating resources required for a particular job, and I had over-committed to projects we couldn't really afford. To be honest, *that* was still in me. If I had done such a poor job of setting a pace that I could sustain myself, perhaps I had burned out others, as well. And perhaps I had not been tough enough to do the hard things that would keep us on track. Perhaps I gained too much self-esteem from being close to the staff. I knew it was hard for me to let anyone serve me; I prided myself on doing my share of the grunt work. But that had sometimes kept me from focusing on the things that only I could do. Sobbing silently, I pleaded with God to help me finally to hear what He was trying to say to me about these things—and not just hear, but change.

Even if Esperanza were to fold, was bankruptcy the way to do it? Didn't the Bible say, "Owe no man anything except to love one another"? I prayed that God would forgive whoever in addition to me was responsible for this situation and help them at least to pay off the debts.

However, those were not the big issues. If Esperanza were really God's project, as I so often said, He had the right to close it down. He didn't *owe* us anything. Esperanza had been a gift of His mercy to us and to the people of north Philadelphia. It wasn't as though we *merited* that mercy.

I tried to visualize Esperanza closing. I almost got sick. No other place in Philadelphia routinely integrated spiritual care with medical care. Luisa and Pedro and Meriediana would have been dead by now if God had not touched

---

their lives. Juan and Miguel and several dozen others *were* dead, but they would be in heaven forever because they met God at Esperanza. The Church and the world needed to hear Esperanza's message, proclaimed almost prophetically. And given Philadelphia's health care situation, a whole lot of Esperanza's patients would have a hard time getting *any* care elsewhere.

I knew God *could* save Esperanza. He had done it already so many times. But not every story has a happy ending in this world. Even prophets had been murdered. A few weeks before, my sister's friend's two-day-old baby had died, despite our prayers. My sister-in-law's marriage was breaking up, despite her prayers. A young mother who was a good friend of my parents had just been shot to death on her front porch as she left for work. Lots of good Christians were being tortured and killed around the world. Lots of good Christian ministries had closed for lack of money. God certainly didn't always intervene as I thought He should. There was no *a priori* guarantee that He would save Esperanza this time.

Then it hit me: the real question was not just how to hope when things look bleak, but how to hope when things are *dead*. Because on this planet, death always wins. Each of my patients was going to die, no matter how hard I fought for them. Each of my friends and family members would die. *I* was going to die. Was all hope only temporary, pending death? Or could one hope in the face of death? Suddenly it struck me that hope that cannot survive the test of death is really no hope at all.

◆　◆　◆　◆　◆　◆　◆

My mind floated back over the fifteen years that we had worked on Esperanza. I recalled the theme of those sermons of Ron's which had laid the foundation for Esperanza: God's Kingdom has really begun, even though the battle is not finished yet. He (and others) had often described the Kingdom of God in terms of World War II. After D-day, though a lot of fighting remained, there was no doubt about the outcome. In the same way, Ron said, Christ's coming was a kind of D-day. Now we are in an in-between age. The Kingdom is *here now*—in tangible, real form, with miracles and divine interventions. And it is also *not yet here now*—many miracles *don't* happen. God sometimes doesn't intervene as we wish He would to remove the immediate consequences of our sin—or even of Adam's and Eve's. He doesn't instantly heal every disease and calm every tornado. He still gives free choice to abusive parents and oppressive societies. But when Jesus died and rose from the dead, God began a work that will eventually defeat evil, and He will see it through to completion. And He is doing that work through us, as we demonstrate His reign in our own spheres of influence.

Furthermore, I recalled, Jesus had behaved as if the goal of the Kingdom now was not to solve the world's problems, but to help us believe in and prepare ourselves for the coming consummation of the Kingdom, which *would* solve the world's problems. His followers had concluded that they had been given *enough* data about the reality of the future kingdom to stake their lives on it. Apparently, so had we—if we had eyes to see.

I, of all people, could not argue with that. Even if Esperanza were to die in the next couple of weeks, I—and *many* people from North Philadelphia—had seen clear evidence that God reigns, and He is very concerned about the health and salvation of poor people. Through incident after incident, we had seen that God is alive, loving, wise, and more powerful than any evil. Every time God mercifully supplied a need, changed a situation, and healed a body or mind or relationship, He poured a little bit more of His love into our hearts. For us, it was only reasonable to keep trusting God with our lives, and to submit ourselves to His rule. It was a rational response for us to hope in God's future reign.

Ultimately, that was the *only* source of hope in the face of death. If Esperanza had helped people lay hold of *this* hope, it had done something very important.

I realized that, whether or not Esperanza survived, my time there had already been a good investment that had yielded a dividend of hope: hope that God is really there, whether or not He answers prayer the way I want Him to; hope that His kingdom is more real than the tangible world I see around me.

I turned on the light on my nightstand and flipped open my Bible. Paul's words to the Romans jumped out to me:

> *"Hope does not disappoint, because God has poured out His love into our hearts by the Holy Spirit, whom He has given us."*[47]

I riffled over a few pages and read from II Corinthians,

"we fix our eyes not on what is seen, but on what is unseen. For what
is seen is temporary, what is unseen is eternal."[48]

That radical statement had galvanized hundreds of thousands of
Christians as they faced lions, flames, and firing squads. It had fortified my
friend Juan DeJesus as he fought the AIDS pneumonia that eventually took
his life. It had strengthened my patient Naomi after her only son was mowed
down by drug lords. It was guaranteed to revolutionize the life of anyone
who believed it.

I wiped my eyes one last time, turned off the lamp, and slipped under
the covers next to Ron, who was snoring gently. "OK, God, I will trust you,
no matter what happens to Esperanza. But if you pull Esperanza through
this one, then I really will write that book."

---

[47] Romans 5:5
[48] II Corinthians 4:18

Resurrection 14

T he letter from Leo and Steve arrived a few days later.

> *"The ministry of Esperanza Health Center has reached a major turning point in the battle we engage in daily. Because of the present health care and funding environment, <u>we presently have no funds to meet our immediate obligations</u>.... The board is and must continue to responsibly investigate all of its options, including dissolution. This is our moral and legal duty. Just as a family requires a steady source of income to thrive, we need hundreds to consider not only a one-time pulse of support, but regular interval contributions in whatever amount seems feasible, no matter the size. We critically need your prayers for a miracle and your assistance as the Lord leads."*

I groaned inwardly. I found Ron in his study and watched him wince as his eyes moved down the page. It didn't matter if Esperanza had plans for reorganization. Who would give money to an organization in that kind of shape?

My heart was still heavy the next morning as I headed to church for women's Bible study. Under any circumstances, that was a good place to bring a heavy heart: those women shared deeply, loved practically, and prayed fervently. That morning I was especially touched by some of the Bible passages we read together:

> *"Be strong in the Lord, and in His mighty power.... For our struggle is not against flesh and blood, but against the rulers, against the authorities, against the powers of this dark world and against the spiritual forces of evil in the heavenly realms...."*[49]

---

[49] Eph. 6:10,12

"Devote yourselves to prayer, being watchful and thankful...."[50]

"This is the confidence that we have in approaching God: that if we ask anything according to His will, He hears us. And if we know that He hears us—whatever we ask—we know that we have what we asked of him...."[51]

I couldn't exactly define God's will, but I felt renewed encouragement to pray. That week I had several rich times of prayer as I lifted Leo and Steve and the other board members to God. As I did laundry the night of the board meeting that would decide Esperanza's fate, I found myself praising God for His goodness and mercy—which would remain whether or not Esperanza stayed open.

Bryan called the next morning with wonderful news. A board member, seeing no good alternative source of high quality care for the whole person in North Philadelphia, had approached his boss, Michael Cardone. Mr. Cardone, a prominent Christian businessman, had promised to give Esperanza $50,000 by the end of the week, and another $10,000 per month for the next year! On the strength of that promise, the board voted to defer bankruptcy for three weeks, giving time to prepare a plan for cutbacks and further fundraising.

During those three weeks, Nancy Hansen, who had been on the board for several years, took action on her own. She was furious about the doomsday letter. I didn't blame Steve. He had worked diligently for years as board president, trying to keep this ship afloat, and he was exhausted. He honestly didn't see any alternative. Nor did some other board members who had worked equally hard. But Nancy felt they had betrayed the trust of the staff and community.

As she often had done before, Nancy wrangled another $50,000 grant from the Huston Foundation, of which she was Vice President. This time, however, the grant was specifically designated to enable Esperanza to hire a consultant to evaluate the situation and make recommendations for the ministry's long-term survival. After hearing her proposal, the board tabled the bankruptcy idea for the time being. Worn out and pessimistic, Steve and several other board members wished Esperanza well and resigned.

---

[50] Col. 4:2
[51] I John 5:14,15

Before they did, however, they approved a first cutback that hit me like a nuclear shock wave. They let both Ted and Leo go, with the understanding that, for the time being, their positions would be consolidated into one, and that neither had the gifts to carry both sets of responsibilities.

And who would? That struck me as a tall order! I hurt for my dear friends Ted and Leo, who had given much to Esperanza. Ted actually stayed on part-time for the next five months to help with the transition. But it sobered me to realize that once he was gone, Esperanza would be functioning with none of its original players. What would happen to its vision?

Now board president, Nancy telephoned Bonnie Camarda, the talented Latina administrator of Living Word Community who had helped me get Esperanza started more than a decade ago. Bonnie had a long and distinguished history of community service and was respected by leaders throughout Philadelphia's Latina, church, business, and philanthropic communities. She also had an M.B.A. from the prestigious Wharton School of the University of Pennsylvania. Bonnie instinctively understood Esperanza's vision. Throughout the years she had assisted informally whenever she could. Nancy convinced the church to allow Bonnie to work half-time as Esperanza's Acting Executive Director for most of the next year – at the church's expense.

◆ ◆ ◆ ◆ ◆ ◆ ◆

Nancy also brought in her consultant, who immediately focused on the billing and accounting departments. I knew a lot of bills had not been getting out. Those departments were doing their best, but apparently employees lacked the skills necessary to handle the stormy and ever-changing waters of multiple managed care plans, Medicare, and Medicaid. In addition, Esperanza's outdated computer system simply couldn't do what was needed, and there had been no money to buy another system. The consultant recommended changes in billing personnel. Those changes helped a little. She and Bonnie also decided to try getting around computer problems by contracting with an outside billing agency.

Next, the consultant looked at the accounting system, which also was outdated, though Ted made it work for him. They brought in an accountant from a temporary agency to develop a better picture of Esperanza's finances.

Having saved many failing secular businesses from the brink, the consultant then turned to the doctors with what seemed to them to be "guns blazing, making early indictments." She was appalled at how long they spent with patients. For their part, they felt utterly frustrated that she had no medical background, and seemed not to understand Esperanza's mission. As time went on, both sides learned from each other. She discovered the staff had many healthy ideas for improvement. She also helped them learn better techniques of coding and documentation of each visit, so they could receive more reimbursement from insurance companies.

On the cost side, Bonnie and the consultant looked for new ways to make cuts. They switched to a less expensive (and less beneficial) health insurance plan for the staff, found a slightly less expensive malpractice insurance carrier, negotiated payment plans with creditors, and searched for outside means for getting the doctors' medical school loans paid off.

The most painful cost-saving measures involved cutting staff. Andrea Daft, Esperanza's brilliant, committed, and compassionate head nurse, left on her own, totally drained. No one faulted her, for she had carried more than her share of the emotional burden for patient and staff needs for four years. In addition to Ted and Leo, three other staff members—a nurse, a counselor, and a social worker, were laid off. In any organization, layoffs are difficult. At Esperanza, where there were spiritual as well as emotional ties, they were particularly painful. Bonnie confided to me later how much it hurt her to have to make those decisions.

Despite her own pain, she worked very hard to keep up staff morale. She bought bagels for everyone on many mornings and made sure the staff's time for daily devotions together was not violated. She regularly invited local and visiting pastors to speak words of faith to the staff. She walked the halls, stopping to talk to one staff member or another, listening to their concerns, affirming them, encouraging them, finding ways to support them personally.

Whether through Bonnie's care or through some kind of divine purification, the difficulties drew the staff together. Six months before, relationships between different groups had been somewhat troubled. Accusations of unfairness, lack of understanding, and racial prejudice had colored tense exchanges. Suggestions for change had often brought defensiveness. Some people felt Esperanza consumed them. They had no time for a social life, and their sacrifices were not appreciated. Some staff members were uncomfortable sharing devotions with others whose worship style and theology were different. Now, those issues had vanished. One receptionist – someone who had vigorously defended her rights in the past – actually volunteered to be laid off rather than see Esperanza go under. Staff members who had teetered on the edge of burn-out found renewed vision and strength in God.

Bonnie also brought in fresh players. Her first coup was convincing Mary Ann Haynes to join the Esperanza team as a fundraiser. Mary Ann, a gifted grant writer, had worked in the business and foundation world for many years. Her proposals to foundations and corporations soon produced some sizeable contributions. In addition, her newsletters to Esperanza's mailing list helped keep a steady stream of private donations flowing into Esperanza's coffers.

A few months later, Bonnie talked John Schaeffer, a leader in Living Word Community, into giving up his lucrative job as nursing supervisor in a large hospital to become managing director of Esperanza. John served as office manager, head nurse, medical director's right hand, Bonnie's representative at any community meetings she couldn't attend, and whatever else was needed. His stint at Esperanza brought a new level of order and efficiency.

Over the next year Bonnie also recruited seven new board members. Their fresh energy and vision would be critical for Esperanza's future.

To top it off, she instigated a face-lift for Esperanza. Eight years after opening day, she heard the walls hollering for new paint. She found individuals and churches willing to underwrite specific projects, such as new carpet for the waiting room. A volunteer even polished the exam room floors until they sparkled.

◆　◆　◆　◆　◆　◆　◆

One day in late October, my telephone rang in Indiana. It was Bonnie.

"You want to hear something wild?"

"Sure! You know me. I'm always up for crazy stuff."

"We just heard that we've been selected to win the SmithKline Beecham Community Health Impact Award for our leadership in immunizations for kids!"

"You've got to be kidding!"

I knew about the SmithKline Beecham award. It was given annually to ten of Philadelphia's non-profit organizations that impact their communities and are nimble, proactive, committed, and effective in their work.

"This means that SmithKline Beecham thinks we are one of the ten most effective non-profit health care providers in Philadelphia!" Bonnie continued. "Let me read to you what their CEO, Jan Leschly, says. 'These exemplary groups who are providing quality healthcare to their communities....are showing the way by exhibiting new, leading healthcare practices that can be adopted by others.' And they're going to give us $40,000 that we can use any way we want to!"

"Incredible! God be praised!" I whooped.

Seven months after almost going bankrupt, and everyone knowing that, we are now considered among the best? Or could it be that God simply wanted Philadelphia to know that He still raises the dead?

After the presentation, one of the SmithKline officials took Bonnie out to lunch to ask her more about this God that Esperanza talked so much about....

◆   ◆   ◆   ◆   ◆   ◆   ◆

By the following summer, Nancy and Bonnie recognized that Esperanza's need for a full-time executive director couldn't be postponed much longer. Nancy asked Mary Beth Swan, who owned her own health care consulting firm, to aid in the search.

I was surprised to hear a couple of months later that Mary Beth herself had been unanimously elected by the board as executive director. She was white; she spoke little Spanish; she had not worked in the inner city. Whatever her skills might be, how could she possibly be effective?

Talk about prejudice! How quickly was I proven wrong!

Mary Beth was a bit surprised to find insufficient funds on hand to cover her first payroll. Her response, however, surprised *me*. She quickly rustled up the money from relationships cultivated outside of Esperanza. Then she declared she would not accept a salary until the rest of the staff were paid, *and* Esperanza was caught up on its bills. I found out later she was *not* independently wealthy. In fact, her husband was laid off during part of that time. Nonetheless, she lived that way for many months.

She also dived into Esperanza's books with a vengeance. She discovered some of Esperanza's quarterly cost reports had not been properly filed with the state. From these reports the state should have reimbursed Esperanza the difference between what Medicaid paid and the actual costs of delivering care to Medicaid patients. She researched and reconstructed those reports and began to file them. Then she began regularly calling the state Medicaid office, congressmen, senators, and the governor's office to urge that they process them quickly.

Meanwhile, determined to account for every penny coming into and going out of Esperanza, she scrutinized the billing and accounting systems. The agency contracted for billing was not performing up to Mary Beth's expectations. By her third month at Esperanza she had secured a brand new computer and software system, courtesy of the Templeton Foundation, to enable her to bring billing back in-house. This time she made sure the billing personnel were well trained and supported.

She also found new accountants. Dr. Hollinger's parents were willing to oversee an improved accounting system. Annual audits by an outside firm since opening day had confirmed that Esperanza's books had been kept faithfully and honestly. Nonetheless, it was heartening to hear that Esperanza's accounting was being done in a cutting-edge manner would meet or exceed the standards of any for-profit business. Esperanza's letterhead would soon bear the seal of the Evangelical Council for Financial Accountability.

Mary Beth delighted in turning expenses into revenue. With a few phone calls and completed applications, she saw Esperanza's doctors qualified to have their medical school debts picked up by Project Medsend, an international agency. By making a few more phone calls and giving a few more guided tours through Esperanza, she procured donations of new equipment for most of the exam rooms, new copiers, new office furniture, and other tools.

Even more important, Mary Beth seemed to be some sort of magnet for talent. Somehow she managed to tap the extraordinary expertise of volunteers from a wide spectrum of disciplines, from marketing and finance to computers and information systems. A clinical psychologist of high repute donated nearly two hundred hours of supervision and training to Esperanza staff. A volunteer psychiatrist, something for which I had prayed desperately for years, began to see Esperanza patients on site regularly. A new optometrist replaced Dr. Foedisch, who had retired after many years of faithful volunteer service at Esperanza.

◆ ◆ ◆ ◆ ◆ ◆ ◆

Less than three years later, Esperanza's full time doctors numbered six, with eleven volunteer docs and new support staff supplementing them. Mary Beth even recruited Dr. Wags, a non-allergic, non-shedding, highly trained therapy dog, who instantly made vaccinations less painful for kids and helped even the sickest adults to smile. Mary Beth did not claim credit for this influx of help. Other staff members contributed to the recruitment process, and all of them gave the credit to God. Nonetheless, Esperanza's strength was growing in many areas.

Affirmations began rolling in. Early in 1999 the Health Federation of Philadelphia released the results of its 1998 audit of Philadelphia's eleven community health centers. Esperanza came in first in every category— from highest patient approval rating and compliance to lowest costs and hospitalizations to best utilization of community resources. About the same time Dr. Ramon Gadea was chosen to receive the Governor's Award for Internal Medicine Excellence for the entire state of Pennsylvania.

But despite the diligence of Mary Beth and others, the money the government owed to Esperanza was *not* rolling in. There was no assurance that the more than $300,000 which the state office admitted was due to Esperanza would *ever* be paid. It did seem strange that, of Pennsylvania's fifty-two federally qualified health centers, the only two that had not received reimbursement were a Christian center in Pittsburgh and Esperanza.

Mary Beth sent a memo to staff, letting them know there was no promise if or when money would come from the state, even though it was due. Did they still want to "stand in the gap" and wait? One hundred percent of the memos came back affirmative, despite car repossessions and eviction notices. In fact, the staff began coming in a half hour earlier to pray together.

Several paydays marched by without checks, taunting receptionists and physicians alike. Finally the board decided that, if funds were not received by June 30, 1999, Esperanza would have to close.

When she called the state office the morning of June 30, an official told Mary Beth that Esperanza would not receive that money any time soon. Bureaucratic procedures kept them from making any promises. Additionally, if ever the money should be released, it certainly would not be wired. Money was never wired, except to health maintenance organizations. Esperanza would just have to wait. At 2:45 she finally brought up her word processor to type a memo to staff and board, informing them that even after months of daily phone calls and interventions by congressmen, senators, and the governor's office, there was still no money. Esperanza would have to close.

At 2:50 the phone rang. The head of Esperanza's division of the department of public welfare informed Mary Beth that $78,000 had just been *wired* into Esperanza's account. The rest of the money would be sent by September!

Thus it was that in September, 1999, Esperanza Health Center was debt-free for the first time since the Robert Wood Johnson Foundation grant expired.

That same September, its lease expired. Esperanza moved to a spacious and attractive new site in the medical office building of Parkview Hospital a few miles away. No one was afraid to drive through this new neighborhood, and Latinos were moving in. It was a nurturing location where Esperanza could stabilize and grow. But it was not where they ultimately wanted to be. Too many of the poorest patients, those who needed Esperanza most, could not get there from the *barrio*. Even while paychecks were still missing, staff and board began discussing a capital campaign to buy or build a facility back in the *barrio*.

◆　◆　◆　◆　◆　◆　◆

I visited Esperanza for their 10-year anniversary celebration in December, 1999. Before the party I walked through the health center with Mary Beth. Improvements were obvious all around me. A volunteer pediatrician who had returned to Esperanza after several years of absence confided to me, "This is a totally different place than it used to be!" Conversations with several people indicated that better efficiency in patient care was not destroying doctors' opportunities to minister to patients. I marveled at Esperanza's formal strategic plan for fundraising and development, as well as plans for a wireless network of portable computers, a full-time chaplain, more social workers, dentistry, and expanded HIV care.

That evening over Puerto Rican delicacies, patients, staff and board members from various eras, and friends of Esperanza shared memories—

some funny, some poignant, all reflecting an awe of how much God had brought them through. I felt a bit overwhelmed to hear how God had preserved the vision that birthed Esperanza so many years ago, even though none of the original players were still present. I would later be even more overwhelmed to learn that Esperanza finished the next year with more revenue than expenses, for the first time in history.

God had indeed raised Esperanza from the dead—to a better life than it ever had before. Esperanza was well on its way to becoming a state-of-the-art health center, on a par with any other health center in the country, but still with an extra dimension. I sat quietly on the plane on the way home, trying to appear normal in case my seatmate should glance sideways from his magazine. But inwardly I was singing at the top of my soul.

If God had raised Esperanza from the dead, what could He not do? It would be insane for me not to trust Him with my own life and the lives of those dear to me, whether or not He was answering my every prayer the way I wanted Him to. This resurrection testified to another resurrection some two thousand years before, which had given an *esperanza, a hope* to all mankind, a hope that superceded death.

The wonder was not that God could make such a magnificent health center, but that He could use what Esperanza used to be. Embarrassment swept over me when I thought about the hundreds of thousands of dollars of reimbursement for which we had not even billed the state; about the inefficiencies we had institutionalized; about the lacks of expertise we had demonstrated in so many ways.

Nevertheless, God chose to use me and my friends—not because we were good, but because we were available. Children were growing up healthy, with all their shots, because I had an office for Bill Pearson to walk into. Old women, imprisoned all of their lives by depression, were free and happy as a result of counseling and treatment they received at Esperanza. Hypertensives and diabetics now controlled their blood pressures and sugars because someone cared enough to work with them in their language. Drug addicts were now clean and sound in body because Esperanza docs and nurses supported them. Brothers and sisters with AIDS now waited for me in heaven, because they met Jesus at Esperanza. Even a pharmaceutical rep and a foundation officer had come to faith in Christ through Esperanza. Across town, a hospital surgeon who shared in the care of one of our difficult patients had said, "Well, I guess we have to begin loving her the way you all do....with God's love." Ripples from our availability had spread far across the pond.

God had worked around more than our lack of skill. My relationships with Him and with others while I was at Esperanza had revealed some serious weaknesses. I had been unrealistic, driven, stubborn, and often difficult to work or live with. But God still used me. Perhaps Esperanza was God's declaration that He would use *anybody* available to Him.

So why would He bother? Suddenly I remembered our daughter, Melody, at age three or four "helping" me bake cookies. Mixing the batter took twice as long, as did kitchen clean-up. But as the cookies emerged from the oven, the joy in her eyes was priceless. Now I had been invited into God's kitchen. The God of the universe had spent quality time with me, and our "cookies" would last for eternity. Despite the messes I had made, God loved me and wanted me to work with Him, in much the same way that I had cherished baking with Melody.

When the time was right, God had also gently let me know that He could run Esperanza without me. It seemed He had set up my time at Esperanza specifically to expose my deep broken places, and then to heal them. I vividly recalled how hopelessly trapped I had felt in my workaholism. How different I felt now! Even though I was back to practicing medicine in Indiana, my life had a healthy balance I could hardly have dared to dream of before.

I pulled my Bible from my backpack and paged over to the first chapter of Ephesians, hoping my seatmate would not see the tears of joy escaping down my cheek. "*I ask...,*" the apostle Paul's words practically glowed, "*that you will know what is the hope to which He has called you.*"[52] So then my experience at Esperanza had been just the appetizer....

---

[52] Eph. 1:18

Epilogue

E arly in 2000 the staff began preparations to put up a mural depicting the
many ways God had intervened in the life of Esperanza, its staff, and
its patients. Years before we had pasted paper "stones of remembrance," on
which were written the specific ways God had provided for us, onto a roll
of shelf paper tacked to a wall. The paper had been taken down when the
wall was painted, and somehow lost. However, Bryan contacted Ted and
me and other former staff to solicit our memories, and little by little the
list was reconstructed. Bryan and his brother and sister constructed and
hung a beautiful frame 4 feet high by 20 feet long in the front entryway. The
Esperanza staff decided to close the clinic on Maundy Thursday, just before
Easter, so they could meet together to put up this Wall of Faithfulness and
commemorate God's goodness.

In mid February, there had been no money for payroll. Mary Beth had
pleaded with the state Medicaid office to release the quarterly wrap-around
reimbursement that had not been paid to Esperanza since early 1999, but had
been told that there was no way to speed up the bureaucratic machinery. She
would simply have to wait for the letter of notification and other paperwork,
and then she could call to find out when the check would be issued. She
should not look for money to be wired; that was never done, except to
health maintenance organizations. Even calls from our state senator's office
availed nothing.

Over the next six weeks there had been no paychecks. Some staff had
their phones turned off, their heat turned off. Some received eviction notices.
Some ran out of food. Staff who still had money shared it with those who
didn't. Others gave what they had: food, or rides to work to save on bus
money. Some individual donors and churches gave special cash gifts to
enable the staff to eat and to take care of each other. No one quit. But the
situation did seem incongruous with our plan to set aside a day to celebrate
God's faithfulness.

Despite this state of affairs, the staff went ahead and closed the clinic on
Maundy Thursday, determined not to let circumstances blind them to God's
unchanging character. They began the morning with praise and worship

and song. Then they put up the individual "stones" in chronological order, beginning with the "call" I had heard from God to start Esperanza in 1982. One by one, each staff member read his or her "stones," in fact shaped like birds and flowers as symbols from Matthew 6 of God's provision, and attached them to the mural. At the end of the afternoon, the group sat without moving, each person's attention riveted on the Wall, intensely aware of God's faithful provision over the years, and of the blessing they had just in knowing Him, even apart from creature comforts.

Finally about 3:30 or 3:45 they broke up. Mary Beth slipped back to her office. On her voice mail a senator's aide had left a message that over $200,000 had just been wired to Esperanza's account—without the preceding paperwork—during the day they had spent giving thanks to God. Could any lesson in thanksgiving be more pointed?

A year later, in February, 2001, Mary Beth calculated that the amount of money still owed to Esperanza by the state and federal governments exceeded a half million dollars. Despite maximal efforts of staff, board members, and sympathetic politicians, the money remained stuck in a bureaucratic quagmire. Without some of that money, Esperanza would again not be able to make the next payroll. A few days before paychecks were due she felt obligated to give staff notice that they were still short, wrote a memo to that effect, and went off to a meeting downtown. While her assistant was stuffing the memo into mailboxes, Mary Beth checked her voice mail from the meeting. Someone had left a message apologizing that a mistake had been made, and money had been wired into Esperanza's account—even though the explanation of reimbursements was not yet available to be mailed out. The amount which had been wired was to the penny what was needed to complete payroll!

I heard these stories shortly after they happened. I liked the miracles, but inwardly I wanted to scream. *God, is this any way to run a health center? Must these poor folk live so close to the edge of the cliff? I know other good Christian organizations that lumber along fairly comfortably, never worrying about meeting payroll. Why couldn't Esperanza be like those? Why must we forever be so out-and-out dependent on You? Why do You always have to make such a point of the fact that You are the One who supplies Esperanza's needs?*

◆　◆　◆　◆　◆　◆　◆

Five years later, Ron and I flew to Philadelphia for a conference, and made arrangements to drop by Esperanza. Staff we had not even met before received us most warmly, invited us to share in morning devotions, and gave us the grand tour. The tour turned out to be a bit of a hug-fest, as I met one after another of the "old warriors" who had stood by me and by Esperanza during the years of great difficulty. The bonds forged while we fought and suffered together had not weakened at all. What a treat it was to sit down with some of them and catch up on personal happenings.

The tour itself revealed a dizzying array of positive changes since my last visit six years previously.

We met new staff with high level qualifications every where we turned. Several new doctors were seeing patients, including one I had mentored briefly 20 years before. We met the HALOS (HIV/AIDS Latino Organization and Services) team, who together were providing outreach to the community and on-going care for approximately 100 people living with HIV. We met new social workers, mental health professionals, nurses, and medical assistants. We chatted with Esperanza's new executive director, Susan Post, a small woman with a big vision and an impressive grasp of the complexities of modern healthcare. We rejoiced to see that her finance and information technology director was a young man who had grown up in the neighborhood. In his brief explanation of what Esperanza would be doing to improve its community relations, I realized what a valuable player he would prove to be to the Esperanza team.

We learned about new programs that had started and new collaborations that had made them possible. Esperanza was now buying common medicines through a federal program and selling them to uninsured patients through a neighborhood pharmacy at a fraction of their wholesale cost. One patient whose anxiety had been difficult to treat had gotten better simply as his wife's huge monthly prescription bill shrank to manageable size. Routine x-rays and ultrasounds had become available to Esperanza's patients on a sliding fee scale basis through an arrangement with Northeast Hospital—one of my dreams come true. Patient education was flourishing as a registered dietitian had joined the nurses and physician assistant who were empowering patients to care better for themselves. Esperanza was participating or getting ready to participate in Project Dulce, of the Philadelphia Diabetes Coalition; an asthma education program of the University of Pennsylvania, a Healthy Heart program tailored to Hispanics by Congreso de Latinos Unidos; and an exercise program sponsored by La Fortaleza, a nearby private physical therapy group.

We discovered down the hall a bit that Esperanza had acquired Tenth Presbyterian Church's Hope Program, which for many years had provided buddy support by volunteers to people living with AIDS in Center City Philadelphia. In the markedly different culture of North Philadelphia Hope's tactics had changed, but its energetic leader was exploiting new openness to HIV education among Afro-American churches, in the youth detention center, and in some public school settings.

To my great joy, we heard that just three months before our visit Esperanza's mental health services had been approved—for the first time ever—to receive Medicaid reimbursement. Two new mental health staff had already been hired, and search had begun for a licensed psychologist. The full-time chaplain for whom staff had hoped for many years was also now on board. He was sensitively following through on the spiritual care that other staff started. Patients had responded overwhelmingly positively to his presence in the health center, and he had helped patients connect with the resources of many of the churches in the area.

These were just the beginning. We heard about the electronic medical records which would be phased in, beginning in a couple of months. No one was particularly looking forward to the headaches that the transition would bring, but all agreed that the increase in efficiency and quality of medical care that would result would be worth the effort. And downstream a year, dental services would begin, to be provided in collaboration with Temple University School of Dentistry. All of the equipment needed for a new dental suite had already been donated.

We also learned that Esperanza had at least a second site. A month before, Esperanza had completed the purchase of an old building back in the heart of the Hispanic commercial district. It would have to be completely gutted and renovated, but it was scheduled to open as a satellite office later in 2006. Strangely, I remembered former executive director Leo Trevino laying hands on that building and "claiming" it some ten years before, long before Esperanza had moved to its present location. As we spoke, staff were also scouting North Philly options for relocating the main office as well, in line with the plans of Esperanza's landlord to use the property differently.[53]

Esperanza was actually considering another potential new "site"—in Ecuador! For years several staff members had individually used their vacations to do mission trips to Latin America. In the fall of 2005, three members of the HIV team traveled to Ecuador, covering all of their own expenses, to teach

50 volunteer health educators how to mobilize their communities to fight AIDS. The phenomenal success of that trip challenged the board to think about Esperanza's role in international health care, particularly in the context of the global AIDS epidemic. Of course, Esperanza couldn't deliver clinical care overseas—that would be better done by locals. However, if Esperanza staff from time to time could share their AIDS experience with health care workers in other countries, they could multiply their impact many-fold. At the time of our visit, a board committee was exploring the direct and indirect effects that international involvement might have on Esperanza.

Finally, we learned about new funding that had made this expansion of services possible. In addition to various smaller grants, Esperanza had been awarded a large federal grant under Title 330. In addition to providing salaries for many of the new staff and resources for new programs, the grant also made Esperanza eligible for greatly reduced malpractice insurance payments—a huge benefit, given the skyrocketing costs of malpractice in Pennsylvania. It was clear to everyone that spiritual care would continue to be done with money raised elsewhere, not this grant money, but that didn't seem to bother anyone. Just as it always had, Esperanza would continue to trust God to supply such money.

As friends drove Ron and me off to our conference that afternoon, I pondered the contrast between the Esperanza I had known and this new Esperanza—financially stable, blossoming on every side, excelling in more ways that I could have imagined. I felt a bit like the Queen of Sheba visiting King

---

[53] In December 2007, Esperanza moved its main office to 3156 Kensington Ave., Philadelphia, PA 19134, while continuing to operate its satellite clinic at 2940 N. Fifth St. As of October, 2010, Esperanza employed 90 staff members, including 17 primary care providers, and offered a host of ancillary services: dental care, medication dispensaries, mental health and social work services, nutrition and dietary counseling, and continued specialized care for patients with HIV. In addition they had restarted the lay health promoter training we had attempted years before, empowering community members to reach out to their neighbors through preventative health education. The Summer Medical Institute had also returned to Esperanza after a gap of several years, as health professions students partnering with local churches conducted door-to-door health and spiritual need screenings with community residents. In December 2009, Esperanza was awarded a $6.5 million Federal grant to construct a new healthcare facility in Hunting Park neighborhood of North Philadelphia. When the new facility opens in late 2011 or early 2012, Esperanza will be able to serve up to 7,000 additional patients. Current information on the health center's programs and people is available at www.esperanzahealth.com.

Solomon more than 900 years before Christ. She had heard about his wisdom and splendor, but nothing had quite prepared her for the reality she saw.

So God is as willing to underwrite success and security as He is life on the ragged edge?

In truth, the intervening years had brought more success to *me* than I would have imagined. Both of my children had gotten excellent scholarships through college and were doing what they most wanted to do. My daughter had found a wonderful husband and had given me three beautiful grandchildren, with a fourth on the way. I had a good job, with partners who would cover for me whenever I needed time off to further an exciting new ministry fighting AIDS globally. My husband and I were happier than at any time in our 38 years of good marriage. We felt the love and support of family and friends and church.

I thought about Abraham, the father of Judeo-Christian and Muslim faiths. He was fabulously wealthy. God apparently did not have a problem granting possessions, status, and influence in abundance. Dared I expect continued prosperity for Esperanza—and myself? Or would life under God's rule sooner or later revert to not knowing till the last minute how the bills would get paid?

Eventually the conversation in the car reached a lull. I slipped my Bible out of my purse on the back seat beside me and looked up God's promise to Abraham.

I swear by myself, declares the Lord, that because you have done this and have not withheld your son, your only son, I will surely bless you.... [54]

Ah, so there was the catch. God had forced Abraham to make a choice between sacrificing on a crude altar the son for whom he had waited for 100 years, in whom was wrapped the entire purpose of his existence, let alone all of his dreams and hopes—versus disobeying the Almighty. God had waited until Abraham was actually bringing the knife down on his beloved child before stopping him, redirecting him to a ram caught in a nearby thicket as the appropriate sacrifice. God didn't mind Abraham having all kinds of

---

[54] Genesis 22:16

blessings—as long as Abraham knew Who reigned supremely and was to be obeyed unwaveringly.

For the moment Esperanza seemed to have passed that test. Many there had obeyed God's call when obedience was costly. Whether it had government grants or not, they would forever remember Who was the source of their paychecks—and of the unique team which had assembled there, the transformations which they observed in patients, and the changes they had seen in the community they served. In the future, as staff would come and go, that lesson would doubtless have to be repeated.

Someday *I* might have to repeat it.

However, whether or not we experienced prosperity at any particular moment was not even the point. We had been given front row season tickets with backstage passes at the Theatre of God's Purposes for the World. We had found riches unrelated to our salaries, riches no amount of money could match, riches more widely available than most people would dream—for those willing to pay the price to get them.

This was definitely the good life....

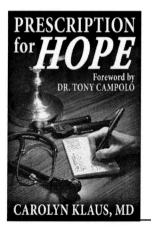

CONTACT AND ORDER INFORMATION

To order additional copies or contact the author
go to **www.hopeworksbooks.com**
or email **hopeworksbooks@gmail.com**
or send this order form with check to
Hopeworks Books, PO Box 1188, Goshen, IN 46527-1188

Number of copies ordered: _____

Total at $13.99/copy: _____

7% sales tax for books shipped to Indiana: _____

Shipping:

☐   First class mail 3-4 days   _____
      First book $3.99
      Each additional book $0.99

☐   Priority mail 2-3 days   _____
      First book $12.98
      Each additional book $1.99

Total: _____

Name _____

Address _____

Phone _____